MY GOD 2 DAY

Dr. Lori Alyse Croom-Bush

I would like to dedicate this book to my favorite professor, the Holy Spirit.

IN LOVING MEMORY OF

Rev. Dr. J.W. Croom, Jr. (my grandfather/first pastor)

Mr. Ronald E. Croom (my dad)

Mr. Jessie Simon (my godfather/mentor/person)

Mrs. Ellease M. Croom (my grandmother/best friend)

Mr. Sam Jones & Mrs. Ruth M. Jones (my grandparents)

ACKNOWLEDGMENTS

I am grateful for the following people/places/things:

Mr. Evan B. Bush (my husband and prayer partner)

Gloria Croom (my mother)

Charity & Christen Jasper (my daughters)

Adrienne M. Nixon (my God-ordained friend)

Randall, Brandon, Elliot, Alexandria, Renita, & Rollin (my siblings)

First Baptist Church Graymont

The Croom, Jones, McHenry, and Simon Families

Spelman College & Hillman College

All Sorors of Delta Sigma Theta Sorority, Inc. & P.R.E.S.T.I.G.E.

NowVision Eye Care

INTRODUCTION

Did we all live the same life? Maybe not, but it definitely seems that way at times. If you were raised by black parents or grandparents, there are certain experiences that probably seemed to be unique to your family at the time. We would later discover that these experiences were actually common throughout the community. This book will use those experiences to point us back to Christ. We will walk down memory lane, laugh, and celebrate our culture all while gaining spiritual insight, encouragement, and Biblical truths to help us strengthen our daily walks with the Lord.

Take this journey with me. Stay committed to devoting daily for the next 26 weeks. Go to your Bible (or Bible App) and open it to the daily scriptures that you see at the bottom of each page. My prayer is that this will become a habit for you with or without my books. Life is so full of distractions. It's easy to drift away and lose focus before you realize it. If we're going to be victorious in this life, we must draw closer to the Lord each day in a world where everything and everyone is competing for our attention. I pray this book will help you do just that. - Lori

DAY 1
TAKE THAT CHICKEN OUT THE FREEZER.

Picture it. You're a kid on summer break, and your mom tells you to do one simple task. She either tells you that morning before she leaves, or she calls from work with the directive. "I need you to take that chicken out of the freezer." It's clearly not a difficult task, yet you get so busy doing nothing that you completely forgot the one thing that this hard-working, bill-paying member of the household asked you to do. It's not until you hear the car pulling up in the driveway and wonder what's for dinner, that your memory is jogged. By then, it's too late, and you know you're in trouble.

I am reminded of the parable of the 10 virgins. Five were wise and five foolish. They were all invited to a wedding celebration. The Jewish custom was for the groom to be escorted into the evening's celebration by guests who were lighting the pathway with their lamps or torches. The groom took longer than expected to reach these 10 virgins, and five of them ran out of lamp oil because they didn't bring any extra to account for a delay. They ran out to buy more oil, but it was too late. When they returned, the groom had already come and taken the five wise virgins into the party. The doors were locked, and the foolish virgins missed the whole thing because they were unprepared. When we forget to take out the chicken, it's often because we thought we had plenty of time to obey, so we didn't make obedience a priority. Are you doing that with God? You don't know when He's going to pull up in the driveway and hold you accountable. Are you really ready to give an account for your actions or lack thereof? Why not obey and prepare as soon as the instructions are given? You know your mama's fried chicken was good! She was only trying to give you something good, and so is God. You don't want to miss out by being foolish and lazy. That's why I'm so glad you're here, starting these daily devotions and spending more time in the word as an act of faith and obedience. I pray these messages will help prepare you for victory on every side.

READ TODAY: MATTHEW 25:1-13

DAY 2
WHEN WE GET IN THIS STORE...

One thing about black parents back in the day...they didn't like to be embarrassed by their children. This led them to give us little "pep" talks before we entered any establishment. Heavy on the quotation marks, because it was really the opposite of pep. Not only did they want us to behave, but they also wanted to help us set realistic expectations for ourselves. They let us know the purpose of the trip and reminded us not to expect any variations. "Now when we get in this store, don't ask for nothing. Don't touch nothing. We are here to get milk and eggs and that's it. Do you understand me?"

Many of our parents set low expectations for us at the store, because they just couldn't afford to go over budget. Jesus, however, did the opposite. He set high expectations for us when He told us the purpose of His trip here to earth. He said that He came so that we could have life and so that we could have it more **abundantly**. Imagine that! Imagine being told that we can enjoy the trip and get not only the things that we need, but also the things that we want! You don't have to walk down the aisle of life with your hands in your pockets, passing sadly by all of the things that are available to others but not to you.

God's blessings of peace and prosperity are available to you in abundance when you follow His will and way for your life. It doesn't mean everything will be easy, but it does mean that you can have everything you need and more to victoriously navigate this crazy world while you're here. Some of us are so used to "lack" that we're walking down the aisle of life with our hands in our pockets, still scared to believe God for more. Newsflash! You were born into a wealthy family the moment you accepted Jesus into your life. We can afford it!

READ TODAY: JOHN 10:10

DAY 3
DON'T ASK FOR NOTHING.

Yesterday, we talked about how our parents prepared us for going inside of the store. One of our instructions was not to ask for anything. I recently came across a social media post where black people were asked to share what "unserious" generational curse they were breaking. One user spoke about how her children *can* ask for something at the store. She said that she keeps a few extra dollars specifically for her kids to be able to get something, whether it be a bag of chips, candy, or a small toy. She went on to say that she doesn't even take them to the store with her if she can't let them get anything. I thought that was cool.

"I don't ask for much." These are words that I found myself saying far too often in relationships. I don't like being a burden to anyone, so I thought that not asking for much was a good quality to have. In a world where men complain about women who are asking them to pay for hair, nails, food, bags, and bills, I prided myself on being "low-maintenance." I think I got so used to asking for little to nothing, that I made people feel comfortable in giving me scraps. One day I woke up and realized that I wasn't asking God for much either. I would pray for others, and rarely ever mention myself to the Lord.

Please don't make the same mistake that I did. You don't get a special trophy from God for not asking for anything. As a matter of fact, that is a trick of the enemy. Satan wants you to feel as if asking God to bless you is selfish. But God's word literally tells us multiple times, in multiple ways to **ask** God. There have been times where I was literally struggling...like...STRUG-A-LING, only to realize that I never actually stopped to ask God to step in and help me. Stop trying to do it all on your own. God can do high-maintenance, easily.

READ TODAY: 1 JOHN 5:14-15

DAY 4
DON'T TOUCH NOTHING.

Yes, we are still with our parents in the store. Our next instruction was always not to touch anything. I'm not going to lie; I use this one with my kids now. I think our parents were trying to protect us here. Being that we were young black children, perhaps they were worried that someone would see us touching something and accuse us of stealing it.

There was a woman in the Bible who reached out to touch something that she feared would get her in trouble. You see, sis had been dealing with an "issue of blood" for twelve years. The Bible doesn't say this, but in my mind, she was on her cycle for 12 years straight…a nightmare. She had been to all kinds of doctors and had spent all her money on co-pays. Well Jesus was passing by in the midst of a crowd, and she took her chances. She reached out and simply touched the hem of His garment, and immediately her "cycle" stopped. Jesus paused and asked who had touched Him. He literally felt the healing power leaving Him. She was scared to respond. Perhaps she felt that she would be accused of stealing her healing from Jesus. Finally, she spoke up and told her testimony of what had just happened. Jesus was not angry at all. He told her to relax, and that her own faith is what helped heal her.

Do you have an issue that you've been dealing with for a long time? Have you tried everything, and nothing seems to work? Do you have a problem that seems unsolvable? The old saints used to say, "Have you any rivers that seem uncrossable?" Well just like we see in today's passage, God specializes in things that seem impossible! Our job is to reach out and make contact with Jesus using our faith. Your faith is your co-pay. Watch what God does when you stop doubting. He may change your situation, or He may change you. He may even change both!

READ TODAY: LUKE 8:43-48

DAY 5
STAY IN OR OUT.

Back in my day, we used to do something very special. It was called going outside. We used to have a time! The neighborhood kids would play together until the sun went down. We had foot races, kickball, basketball, two-hand-touch football, bikes, roller skates, hide-and-seek, hide-and-go-get (I never played that one), and ice-cream trucks! But one thing our parents and grandparents did not allow, was for us to toggle freely between indoors and outdoors. If we were going to be outside, we needed to **stay** outside. It was so serious, that if you came inside for any reason (to pee, get some water, or cool off), you ran the risk of not getting to go back out.

When our parents would say, "Stay in or out!" They really wanted us to make up our minds and stick to it. Well, the Bible also speaks negatively about our ambivalence. It says that a double-minded man is unstable in all his ways. If your life seems to be unstable, ask yourself, "Am I double-minded?" Is it possible that you are trying to have one foot in the door with God and one foot out? I'm not talking about the unbiblical rules and laws that religion tries to stuff down your throat. I'm talking about your heart. Are you fully submitted to God? Or are you still trying to have your own way a lil' bit? Do you do whatever you want to do up until you need something from God? Do you only obey Him when you are desperate for His help? It's okay, you don't have to answer me. It's a book, so I can't hear you anyway. Just take it as food for thought. If our parents didn't like us running in and out of their house, what makes you think God does? Oop...let me back on out of this devotion before I make somebody mad today! Love you, friend.

READ TODAY: JAMES 1:8

DAY 6
RUNNING UP MY POWER BILL...

Yesterday, we talked about how black parents didn't like you running in and out of their house. For a little razzle dazzle, they would add that your opening and closing of their door was letting all the cool air out and running up their power bill. Apparently, a child opening the door for a few seconds was enough to do major damage.

Let's talk about Jesus today. Jesus paid our power bill. You see, we were once lost in sin, and sin has a cost. We voluntarily left the door to our hearts wide open, and let the "cool air" out while allowing the "hot air" in. We ran our own power bill sky high with sin and had no way to pay it. As a matter of fact, our power should have been shut off, but God saw fit to send His own son to pay that bill for us. Jesus paid it all when He took on the penalty for our sins. He suffered, bled, and died on the cross...on a hill called Calvary, so that we could keep our lights on. Not only did He die on that cross, but he also rose again on that third day. And the same power that raised Jesus from the dead, is the same power that we now have access to every day of our lives.

So if you feel powerless, let me tell you...you're not. All it takes is a decision to accept the free gift of power that was given to us by God through Christ Jesus. It is Satan's plan to make you feel guilty and hopeless about a bill that you can't afford to pay. Remove that burden from yourself, because Jesus already paid that debt in full. Let's be grateful today that our "lights" are on, and we still have power.

READ TODAY: COLOSSIANS 1:11-14

DAY 7
STAY IN A CHILD'S PLACE.

Everything is so different now. Back in my day, most adults had clear boundaries when it came to children. They even came up with an invisible location for us to reside and called it, "A Child's Place." Yup, and we had to stay there too. We weren't supposed to listen in on grown folks' conversations, and we definitely weren't supposed to chime in with our thoughts or opinions about what grown folks were doing. To be told "stay in a child's place," was an extremely humbling moment.

As humbling (and sometimes as humiliating) as that moment was, our parents were simply trying to keep us from growing up too fast or thinking that we knew more than we did. And now that we're grown, we don't have to worry about that anymore, right? Not exactly. Jesus still wants us to stay in a child's place, and I'm not talking about that expensive kid's clothing store. Wait…that's The Children's Place. I digress. Listen, Jesus literally says that we need to become like little children to enter the kingdom of heaven. This requires us to humble ourselves. If we are too prideful and too arrogant, we will never admit that we need the Lord. Without humility and a child-like nature, we will never open up our hearts and minds to receive wisdom from God, because we would be too busy thinking we already know it all.

There have been times where I was led by my own crazy, immature ideas instead of staying in a child's place, and allowing my Father to take my hand to guide me. Don't be like me. Don't snatch your hand away from God's hand thinking you're grown and already know the way. He sees and knows the oncoming traffic and is there to guide His children across every street.

READ TODAY: MATTHEW 18:1-4

DAY 8
DO YOU HAVE MCDONALD'S MONEY?

As black children growing up in America, some of us had the bright idea that maybe if we just asked to stop at McDonald's on the way home, our parents would oblige. Being the black parents that they were, however, they just had to be extra. A simple yes or no wouldn't suffice. The black parent handbook must have mandated that they reply with, "Do you have McDonald's money?" They knew we didn't.

As young children, we were already learning that if we really wanted something, we needed to be able to afford it. With God, however, things are the opposite. In Isaiah 55, He invites anyone who is thirsty to come and drink. Anyone, even those without money, are invited to come, buy, eat, and drink of Him. Forget what you've heard. Salvation is **free.** It is a gift given to us by God. He never says, "Do you have salvation money?" Now I know we give and sow our seeds, but the truth is, we could never pay God for the real cost of our salvation. We don't have salvation money! But guess what? We don't need it.

Everyone is charging for everything these days. Heck, this book wasn't even free, huh? But listen, you can change your **entire life** around for free ninety-nine by accepting God's invitation to eat and drink what He offers. It's all outlined in His word, which is also known as the bread of life. The more of it you eat and digest, the healthier your mind and spirit will become. My challenge to you this year is to eat some every day. My job is to use these devotions to point you to the word. Your job is to look up the passages at the bottom of each page and read them. We do so much else, right? Why not make time to accept a free meal from God? His word is the original "happy" meal.

READ TODAY: ISAIAH 55: 1-3

DAY 9
ONE OF YOUR LIL' FRIENDS

Back in the day, our parents commanded a different level of respect. Perhaps there was a time where you got confused and forgot exactly who you were talking to. They were quick to remind us that, "I'm not one of your lil' friends." This meant that we needed to watch what we said and how we said it when it came to them. It was a swift reminder that we couldn't treat the people who fed, housed, and clothed us the same way that we treated our peers out on the playground.

In the book of Numbers, The Bible reminds us that God ain't one of our lil' friends either. I don't want to confuse anyone here. To be clear, God is absolutely a friend to us, but He isn't one of our "lil' friends," and there **is** a difference. Numbers says, "God is not a man, that He should lie...". In other words, He's not just some regular man. When He says something, you can take that to the bank. He doesn't lie, and He doesn't have to go back and apologize for getting it wrong. This sets God apart from anyone else you will ever know or experience on this earth. Yet, we sometimes treat Him like He's going to let us down just like someone else did.

God never promised that you will know exactly why He allows things to play out the way they do, but He did promise that all things will work together for good for those of us who love Him. That being said, He's not one of your lil' friends. He's God with a BIG G...not the little one. Remember that the next time you think that the One who feeds, houses, and clothes you doesn't have your best interest at heart.

READ TODAY: NUMBERS 23:19

DAY 10
BEAT YOU LIKE YOU STOLE SOMETHING

I have no idea the origins of this phrase, but if you grew up black in America, chances are that you have also heard of it. No one likes a thief, so I imagine that anyone in the community caught stealing might catch some serious hands. And since we have to put a little razzle dazzle on everything, this phrase is often used to emphasize just how severe a potential physical altercation would be.

This is the perfect time to tell you about these guys in the Bible known as the "Seven Sons of Sceva." These guys saw where God had been using Paul the Apostle to perform many miracles. Now these guys weren't actually believers or followers of Christ. They were more like self-proclaimed exorcists. One day, they had this bright idea that they could copy what they saw Paul doing and cast an evil spirit out of a man by using the name of Jesus.

You won't believe what happened next! The evil spirit was like, "Hold up now! I know Jesus, and I know Paul, but who the *bleep* are y'all?!" *mink mink mink* The evil spirit that was in the man, leaped onto them, beat them like they stole something, and ran them out of the house, embarrassed and naked. Whew chile! I said all that to say, don't play with God. We see it all the time in churches where people think it's cute to try and copy someone else's anointing. It's too dangerous! You don't want to go toe-to-toe with an evil spirit without the **real** power of the Holy Spirit backing you up. You will get beat like you stole someone else's identity. The best thing is to get to know the Lord for yourself and find out what He has assigned **you** to do and who He has assigned **you** to be. Your gift may not look like anything you've ever seen before, and that's okay!

READ TODAY: ACTS 19:11-16

DAY 11
BOO BOO THE FOOL

Nobody knows exactly who Boo Boo the Fool is or what he looks like, but for some odd reason, black folks love to ask you if they bear any resemblance to him. This question is usually asked in response to someone who is clearly lying or trying to get over on you. If someone says, for example, that they don't know what happened to the leftover cheesecake in the fridge, but that same person has graham cracker crust all around their mouth, the proper African American response would be, "Do I look like Boo Boo The Fool to you?"

The Bible has a lot of things to say about being BBTF. One such thing is found in the book of Proverbs. It says that a fool takes no pleasure in actually understanding anything but would rather air their own uninformed opinions. After reading this description, I'm realizing that I may not know BBTF, but I'm almost certain I've met some of his/her descendants. I don't think anyone reading this book would be a descendant of BBTF though, so I think the best thing to do here is to talk about how to deal with one.

Dealing with a fool is stressful. Stress causes our bodies to release a steroid called cortisol. Cortisol can make you gain weight and get sick. Getting sick can make you die. Dying can make you dead. So what did we learn today? We learned that fools can be hazardous to your health. My advice to you is to search the scriptures and become familiar with the various ways that the Bible describes a fool. Being armed with that knowledge will allow you to recognize one when you see one so that you can place the proper boundaries around your mind, body, and spirit. Have you let a fool get too close to you? Think on these things.

READ TODAY: PROVERBS 18:2

DAY 12
ON CHURCH GROUNDS

January 12th will always be a special day to me. Today is my mom's birthday, so I wanted to use a phrase that I heard her say often. You see, there was a time when people reverenced the church much more than they do now. There were certain things that you just wouldn't do "on church grounds." I thought it was pretty funny that sometimes we'd ride all the way to church listening to the R&B station (thanks, Dad), but as soon as we hit the parking lot, mom would turn down the radio and say, "We're on church grounds now."

Even as a young child, I always wondered to myself, "If it's something you can't do on church grounds, should you be doing it at all?" But as I grew a little older, I learned that the church is much more than just a building or piece of property. I learned that the actual church is not built with bricks, but with people. You and I are the church. "On church grounds" took on a whole new meaning for me. Wherever I am, the church is present. I **am** church grounds. My God Today!

If we are the church grounds, let us be careful to reverence and respect the sacredness that we carry. The Bible says that our body is the temple of the Holy Ghost. We must learn to respect ourselves just as much as (maybe more than) we respect those buildings. This means letting go of anything that could defile us. Respect and protect your mind, body, and spirit, because the Holy Spirit deserves a clean place to dwell. Is the Holy Spirit comfortable living on your church grounds? Can He operate at full capacity within you, or does He have to work around mess, clutter, and pollution? Let's strive today to be better groundskeepers for the Holy Spirit.

READ TODAY: 1 CORINTHIANS 6:19-20

DAY 13
WHAT YOU GOT A TASTE FOR?

There are certain phrases that I honestly never realized were only used by black people. Perhaps other cultures say it, but I've only heard black folks saying it exactly like this. Sure, we could easily just say, "What would you like to eat?" But you know we have to put a little pizazz on everything. So I will pose the same question to you. What you got a taste for?

I don't usually subscribe to stereotypes, but the one about women never knowing what they want to eat may have some validity to it for me. And although we may not know what we have a taste for in the natural, we can't be that way in the spirit. The Bible says that those of us who hunger and thirst after **righteousness** shall be filled. If you are still trying to figure out how close you can get to the line without technically crossing it, you may still be in an immature space spiritually. If you're still trying to figure out exactly how much you can get away with before feeling guilty about it, you might have to ask yourself some tough questions. Why *don't* I want to do things God's way?

When you hunger and thirst for something, you have an earnest desire that leads you to action. Think about it. When we get hungry or thirsty, we don't just sit there…unless we're broke, of course. Actually, I take that back…even broke people come up with a plan. If you truly have a taste for righteousness, you will come up with a plan and take some action to do things the way God wants them done in your life. Did you know that some people don't read the Bible or pray simply because they don't want the Holy Spirit to convict them about something wrong that they don't want to stop? We all mess up sometimes, but it's dangerous when you don't even have a taste for righteousness.

READ TODAY: MATTHEW 5:6

DAY 14
THE HAWK IS OUT.

Does anybody know what this one means? I used to hear my dad say it. I have no idea what an actual hawk has to do with anything, but this is what some black folks will say when they walk outside and it's cold and windy. If the hawk is out, it typically means that a strong wind has blown past every layer of clothing you have on and has chilled you to your core.

Life is so unpredictable at times. Perhaps you woke up one day and received some unexpected news that shook you to your core. Perhaps it was like a bone-chilling wind that blew through your life causing massive disruption. If you live long enough, you will surely experience the hawk. But have you ever noticed how different people can go through similar things but with totally different outcomes?

In Matthew, Jesus describes the difference between a wise man and a foolish man. He says the wise man built his house upon a rock. When the rain and wind beat on the house, it stood tall because of its strong foundation. The foolish man, by contrast, built his house on sand. When the rain and wind beat on that house, it was completely devastated and utterly destroyed. The only difference is what those houses were built upon. I just love how plainly Jesus used to make things.

Today, I just want to encourage you to build your life upon the solid rock that is Jesus. Society will have you thinking your foundation is good looks, money, cars, clothes, careers, or a love life. But when the hawk is out, none of that stuff can withstand. It can all be blown away in an instant. Even the earth itself has tectonic plates just a shiftin' and a slippin'. Only the true and living God is strong enough and to be your firm foundation. Everything else is sinking sand.

READ TODAY: MATTHEW 7:24-28

DAY 15
DOWN LIKE FOUR FLAT TIRES

If someone has been your friend since kindergarten, spent the night at your house more times than you can count, covered for you when you skipped class, introduced you to your current husband or wife, and is the godparent to your firstborn child, you might let it be known that you and that person are down like four flat tires. In other words, y'all are pretty close.

But what happens when it's the middle of January, the holidays are over, your Christmas tree is (probably) down, it still gets dark early, and it's cold? There is a real possibility that you may begin feeling down like four flat tires, but not in a good way. If you are feeling sad, I just want to take a moment to encourage you. Sometimes when you're feeling down, the best thing to do is to start thanking God for as much as you can think of. There is **always** something to be grateful for, even in the tough times.

In the 42nd Psalm, David was talking about how he had been depressed. His solution to get out of his funk was to "remember" how God had been there for him in previous places. David had a lot to be down about, but he weaponized his own memory of God's goodness and used it in the battle for his mind. You see...if the devil can get you to forget how good God has been to you in other places, he can keep you feeling sad and sorry for yourself just as long as he wants to. Don't fall for it. If you have to keep a journal to remember God's blessings, do it! Go back and recall how He fought for you and won. Your memory will help you to inflate those tires again and roll on to your next destination in God.

READ TODAY: PSALMS 42:6

DAY 16
GO ASK YOUR DADDY.

Being a parent is exhausting. I know that now. And if you grew up in a two-parent household, you may have witnessed the occasional shifting back and forth of responsibilities between mom and dad. When you asked your mom for something (help, permission, advice, etc.), she would occasionally shoo you away by telling you to go ask your daddy. When you went to go ask your daddy, his first response would usually be, "Ask your mama." There was great disappointment on dad's face when we would respond, "I did. She told me to ask you."

Aren't you glad that our Heavenly Father does not have any problems taking responsibility for His children? Aren't you glad that God doesn't get tired and shovel you off on some less qualified entity? You can't ask God for too much help, for too much permission, or for too much advice. If you want to live a life within God's will, you're going to have to make going to "ask your daddy" a daily occurrence. Our Father is concerned about everything that concerns us, so we should bring it all to Him.

Some of life's difficulties are unavoidable. But there are so many unnecessary struggles that we face simply because we don't acknowledge God first and wait for His instructions to guide us. Sometimes we get in a rush and decide to go with whatever idea feels best at the time. We try to take a shortcut and end up having to go a much longer route than if we had gone to God first and been patient. God is so patient with us, but we struggle being patient with Him. Let's do a better job of asking Him for our needs and waiting (with a good attitude) while He comes through for us.

READ TODAY: JAMES 4:2

DAY 17
RIPPIN' & RUNNIN'

Sure…we could say, "I've got some errands to run." But "I've got some rippin' and runnin' to do…" just sounds so much better! I love this one. Somebody who has to rip and run, has multiple places to be, multiple people to see, and multiple tasks to complete. This is another phrase that I grew up hearing on a regular basis, not knowing it was a black thang.

Well the Bible speaks of rippin' and runnin' too! Hebrews chapter 12 starts off by telling us to lay aside sin (and any other thing that weighs us down) so that we will be able to run life's race with patience. If you've ever watched an Olympic track meet, I'm sure you've noticed that their attire doesn't have much fabric. The women's track outfits are literally one step above a two-piece bathing suit. That's because when it comes to winning the race, every millisecond matters. They can't have anything that will contribute to their wind "resistance".

So what about you? Do you have things that are contributing to your resistance? Are there things, people, habits, or mindsets hanging on to you and making your race unnecessarily difficult? It's time to rip them off so you can run! I think about those tear-away warmup suits we used to have in high school sports. When the coach calls for you, you better be ready to rip those warmups off and run into the game! Well if you didn't already know, God is calling you off of the bench and into the game. And if you stay ready, you won't have to get ready. Begin to pray and ask God for the wisdom to know which things in your life should be ripped away. You can even ask Him for a strategy on how to best move on from those things. God will answer you because He wants to see you running an excellent race and winning in your lane.

READ TODAY: HEBREWS 12:1

DAY 18
FINNA

I hope nobody is confused about this one, but let me use it in a sentence just in case. "I'm **finna** run to the store. Y'all need anything?" The word "finna" is an abbreviated black version of the phrase, "fixing to." This is the southern way of saying, "I'm getting ready to..." When you are "fixing" to do a thing, it means you are in a preparation phase for the task at hand.

When you set out to accomplish something, how do you prepare? Or do you even prepare? Do you make rash/spur of the moment decisions that are driven by your emotions? Or do you sit down with God and get His strategy first? Let me go over a few steps you can use to determine how to do what you are finna do.

1. Pray. Ask God to make His will on the matter clear and obvious.
2. Calm yourself and listen for God. It's hard to hear when your mind is in a chaotic state. Try to step outside of the emotions.
3. Find out what the Bible says about it. God isn't going to have you doing anything that opposes His established principles.
4. Consider the consequences of your actions.
5. Pray more. Ask God to give you a strategy so that you can go about it in the right way, with integrity, and in His timing.
6. Fast if necessary. If you continue to have conflicting/confusing thoughts, fasting will lower the volume of your flesh and allow you to operate more easily with your spirit.
7. Have patience. If you feel you have to rush into something quickly before understanding God's will, that is a trick from Satan.

READ TODAY: LUKE 14:28

DAY 19
HOW MUCH THAT SET YOU BACK?

Asking someone how much something set them back was another way of asking how much something cost. "I really like that watch man. How much that set you back?" You don't hear this phrase much anymore, perhaps because it's considered bad manners to flat out ask someone how much they paid for something. You should just be like me and google it to find the price!

Anyway, I know I said it was rude to ask someone what they paid, but in today's devotion I'm going to be rude and ask. How much did **that** set you back? You see, when we say something has set you back, it means that some of your progress has been negated by that action or decision. In what area had you been doing well up until you allowed something to come along and set you back to the starting line? Perhaps you had been controlling your temper well, but an argument with your spouse set you back to a place you thought you were past. Perhaps you had been eating right, but Thanksgiving through Christmas came along and set you back to your poor eating habits which caused you to regain all the weight you lost. Perhaps you had determined to focus on improving yourself, but you allowed some man or woman to come along and set you back to your old ways.

Listen. I just want to encourage you today not to give up. Just because you experienced a setback, does not mean you have failed. I'm guilty of saying, "Welp...I already messed up, might as well keep going with this peach cobbler!" Don't be like me. Even the apostle Paul talks about his struggles with doing what's right. Satan wants you to think your setback is a good enough reason to quit trying. Don't fall for that! Dust yourself off and keep going my children!

READ TODAY: ROMANS 7:15-8:1 (TLB)

DAY 20
Y'ALL NOT HOT?

I love this one, and I am guilty of using it to this day. I don't know what it is about black people's DNA that makes us want to first determine if our hotness is a shared experience. Instead of just stating that we are hot, we have to figure out why no one around us seems to be as uncomfortable as we are. Surely it's not just me that's hot!

You already know I'm going to ask y'all the same question. Y'all not hot? When it comes to your relationship with the Lord, let me break it down to you in wing flavors. Are you mild, medium, or hot? The interesting thing is that God has a preference. God would prefer you to be mild or to be hot, but if you are medium, He can't stand that and will spit you out! Mild wings are mild. Hot wings are hot. But what is medium really? It's trying to be both mild and hot at the same time, and therefore doesn't have its own distinct identity. Like…what is medium trying to do with my tastebuds? I need it to decide.

And that's what God is saying to us. If you really have taken the time to get to know God, you can't help but be passionate about Him. I mean…God is absolutely amazing! Have you ever been a relationship with someone who never really took the time to see how dope of a person you are? They couldn't love you how you needed to be loved, and they couldn't get as excited about you as they needed to get. That is the worst. Either be down for me all the way, or leave me alone. Don't have me in some holding pattern of your mediocre feelings towards me. We all want someone who can be hot for us, so let's not be medium with God. Spend more time with Him, study His word, and watch your passion for Him grow!

READ TODAY: REVELATION 3:16

DAY 21
WHO ALL OVER THERE?

Who all over there? This is such a fair question. It's what black people ask before they decide whether or not to accept an invitation to someone's get-together. Knowing who is already over there is the critical determining factor. Do I know any of those people? Do I like any of those people? Are any of those people fun to be around? Are those people safe to be around? Will something pop off?

We should keep this same energy with the rest of our lives as well. Everybody is not deserving of your presence. "You are the company you keep." This is an old saying that warns us to be careful about who we spend our time with, lest we become just like them. It is true that hanging around the wrong crowd can be dangerous and detrimental. Bad influences are real, but sometimes they are subtle.

The Bible tells us that we are blessed when we do not allow the ungodly to have an influential place in our lives. It's a good idea to take inventory over "who all over there" in your life. Are there voices over there that don't line up with God's voice? Are there influences over there that cause you to go in the wrong direction spiritually? My prayer is that you become strong enough in your spiritual walk to be a good influence on others and not the other way around. But use wisdom, know your limitations, and set boundaries.

READ TODAY: PSALM 1:1

DAY 22
CPT

CPT (also known as CP Time) is an abbreviation for Colored People's Time. I don't know who made this one up, but it has been around for a really long time, and virtually all black people in America know what it means. We've all been to a wedding or some other event that was set to start at 3:00 but didn't start until 3:49. This event was running on CP Time.

I must confess that there have been several events that I just knew in my spirit weren't going to start on time. So of course, I showed up late. There's nothing worse than rushing to show up somewhere on time, only for the event itself to be on CPT. Thankfully, we can take great comfort in the fact that God never runs on CP Time, and He never shows up late.

When God gives you a promise or a vision, please understand that He is more than able to start the event on time. We struggle, however, because His timing may not match up with our desired timeframe. We have need of patience. It's God's job to manifest the promise in His perfect timing. It's your job to be obedient and patient while you wait. You're not going speed anything up by complaining and being angry with God. **How** you wait is a true reflection of your faith in God. If we truly believe that He is an all-knowing God, we should trust Him with everything, including the timing.

READ TODAY: HABAKKUK 2:3

DAY 23
THAT'S WHY YA CAR MESSED UP NOW!

Have you ever been driving on the road when you witnessed another car driving recklessly past you? Whenever the reckless car passes and we see that it is beat up or damaged in some kind of way, we shout at the car as if it can hear us. We say, "That's why ya car messed up now!"

It's kind of crazy to think that some people can experience the unfortunate consequences of their own actions, but never think to modify said actions. Okay, let's stop the cap. It's us. We are the "some people." I have personally seen my clothes stop fitting and still ordered the cajun ranch fries along with my wings. We are the reckless drivers who wreck but keep driving recklessly.

Sometimes we just need to get real with ourselves and admit that it's not just the devil attacking us and making things hard. Sometimes we make things hard on ourselves by refusing to do better in certain areas. I am grateful for God's grace which allows us to be human, but God never said that our actions wouldn't have consequences. As a matter of fact, He said that we would reap what we sow. And for a lot of us, our refusal to do things God's way is exactly "why ya car messed up now." We cannot live in rebellion to God and then be surprised when we do damage to our "vehicle."

Is there anything in your life that you can honestly say is not matching up with who you are as a child of God? Are you dealing with unnecessary pain and difficulty in life because of those reckless things? Pray and ask God to reveal to you the "causes and effects" of where you find yourself in life.

READ TODAY: GALATIANS 6:7-8

DAY 24
THIS DON'T MAKE NO **** SENSE!

I don't know what it is about us as a people, but we do not like to stand in lines. Any time we have to stand in a line for any more than five minutes, we say (either out loud or to ourselves), "This don't make no **** sense!" We then start looking around to the front of the line trying to figure out what the "hold up" is. Anything over five minutes and we are liable to scrap everything and get out of the line all together.

I don't know where we get our lack of patience, but it really isn't good. When the Holy Spirit is at work in your life, you will see certain byproducts being created. Patience is one of those byproducts. Patience is so important, man. Imagine walking off and leaving your entire shopping cart in the grocery store because the line wasn't moving fast enough. That's what some of us do. We throw in the towel before getting everything that we need, simply because we don't want to wait.

Think about Abraham and Sarah in the Bible. They waited so long to have a son, but at some point, they ran out of patience. They came up with an alternate plan that ended up causing generations of turmoil. I don't know who needs to hear this today, but now isn't the time to get out of the line. Don't come up with some alternate plan driven by your desire to rush. Ask the Holy Spirit to help you grow in the area of patience. God sees down the street and around the corner. If there seems to be a delay, He has a reason why!

READ TODAY: GALATIANS 6:9

26

DAY 25
I'M NOT GOOD WITH NAMES.

Okay, let me set this one up for you. Have you ever met someone who graduated from the same high school in the same year as someone else you know? You say, "You were Washington class of 1999? Do you know DaMarcus Williams? He was dark-skinned, played basketball, and drove that black Acura Legend." It's so disappointing when they draw a blank. Like...how in the world could they be Washington '99 and **not** know DaMarcus Williams? That's when they hit you with "Yeah...I'm not good with names."

Aren't you glad that God is good with names? Out of over 7.8 billion people on this earth, God not only knows your name, but He knows literally everything about you. The Bible says that He even knows the number of hairs on your head, which is really impressive if you think about it, because that number changes every day! God keeps track of you. His eye is always upon you.

Sometimes, when life gets hard, it's easy to think that maybe God has forgotten about you. Maybe He has forgotten your name. When you look around and see others being blessed while you're struggling, it can make you wonder why God doesn't seem to be moving in your situation. I can assure you that He cares about everything that concerns you and that He has not forgotten you nor the promises that He made to you. You are just as important to God as anybody else, so don't let any temporary circumstance make you doubt that His thoughts and plans for you are good. I hope that you will be encouraged today. Sometimes when I feel that feeling, I will pray and ask God to do something for me, big or small, to show me that He's with me today. It works for me. Sometimes all it takes is for us to ask!

READ TODAY: MATTHEW 10:29-31

DAY 26
I JUST KNOW FACES.

When a black person tells you that they aren't good with names (see yesterday's devotion), it is very often followed by the phrase, "I just know faces." We, as a people, can go years…decades even…knowing a person only by their face. Just this past Sunday, I broke down and asked one of my church buddies what his name was. That's pretty wild considering the fact that we've had several conversations over the past year or so. And now that I'm thinking about it, I wonder if he even knows my name. Well, shout out to Chris if he's reading this. I'm the lady from church who always asks about how your mom is doing.

And now I want us to think about our relationship with the Lord. I'm glad that we know His name, but do we really get to know His face? When we think about someone's face, we think about the unique features that help us identify who they are. God also has unique features that we can use to identify Him and to differentiate Him from anyone else we know. God's "facial" features are absolutely beautiful and yet not fully describable, because it takes more than a lifetime to take it all in. I could go on and on about what I have experienced with God, but by the time I complete this book, He will show me a whole new facet of Himself that I just never knew. That's why you have to establish your own close relationship with the Lord outside of any book or anyone else's accounts.

It's a blessing to be able to recognize the "facial" features of God, because it comes in handy when Satan pops up trying to show his a**. Knowing God makes it easier to identify what is **not** God. We must be careful that we're not constantly seeking His hand for blessings without a passionate desire to seek His face.

READ TODAY: PSALMS 27:8

DAY 27
CLOSED MOUTHS DON'T GET FED.

Y'all are not going to believe this! And I know this isn't my personal diary, but I felt like sharing this today because it's relevant. Remember a couple days ago when I was talking about asking God to send little reminders that He's still present with you? So of course that was my prayer as I was writing. And guess what? A couple of hours after I wrote and prayed that, He did it for me! One of my favorite shows currently on TV is called *Johnson*. (I don't watch much TV, so if I actually follow a whole show, that means I **really** like it.) Last night, I received a surprise video call from three out of the four main characters on the show! We talked for a bit, and I was so excited! Someone who knew I loved the show, set it all up, and I felt very blessed. Thanks Carmen!

I couldn't help but think, "Wow, God! That was quick!" But as the saying goes, "closed mouths don't get fed." That's darn near a Bible verse if you ask me. The Bible puts it more like this, "You have not, because you **ask** not." Over and over, God's word tells us to ask for what we desire and for what we have need of. This is important with God and also in the natural realm. Do you know there are people who would literally rather starve than to ask someone for help? Make it make sense! Oh wait…I'm the writer. That's my job. **It's pride!** Sometimes our foolish pride stops us from asking people for help. That same pride is what makes us think that we can handle everything on our own without God until we are in a full-blown crisis. God is not the "Olivia Pope" of our lives. We don't have to wait until everything is falling apart before we open our mouths to Him. What do you need? It doesn't even have to be an emergency. Open your mouth today and get fed!

READ TODAY: JAMES 4:2

DAY 28
I DIDN'T FALL OFF THE TURNIP TRUCK YESTERDAY.

Have you ever had someone tell you a bold-faced lie? I mean…the lie was so lie-ish, lie-y, and lie-abolical that you couldn't help but feel personally offended by it. The lie was so obviously false that you had to question yourself to figure out what made them think you were dumb enough to try this. One common black response to such a delusion is, "I didn't fall off the turnip truck yesterday, you know." As a young child I would be so confused hearing my dad say this. Turnips? Trucks? Falling? Yesterday? I was lost.

I did a little research on the origin of this phrase, and it all makes sense now. Apparently, people who were wishing to escape the rural/country lifestyle, would sometimes hitch a ride into town on the trucks that were carrying produce to a bigger city. Someone fresh out of the country life would be more naïve and vulnerable to scammers in the city.

And this, my children, is why we have to be more intentional about studying, learning, and growing in God. When we first give our lives over to Christ, we are babes in the faith. We are fresh off of the sinner truck. (Really? The sinner truck? Is that the best thing I can come up with?!) And we have a scammer who is chomping at the bit to take advantage of our lack of knowledge about the ways of God. The devil is always hoping to find and exploit your vulnerabilities. He knows that certain bold-faced lies are more likely to work with someone who doesn't know God's word and who doesn't understand His promises. Knowing this, let us be more intentional about strengthening our faith and learning more about what we say we believe. Reading this devotional and studying the daily scriptures is a great way! Keep going!

READ TODAY: 1 PETER 5:8-11

DAY 29
I WASN'T BORN LAST NIGHT.

This, or a variation of it, is another way of responding to someone who tries to make a fool out of you. My dad would often say, "I may have been born **AT** night, but I wasn't born **LAST** night. If you wanted to get something over on him, you'd have to try harder and step up your game.

Yesterday we talked about how Satan wishes to exploit the vulnerabilities of new believers. Today, however, I think it's important to mention that we have an enemy who is not lazy. Just because it's a little harder to deceive a mature believer, does not stop the devil from trying. If he has to step up his game of lies and manipulation in order to trip you up, he will certainly still try. That's why it's important not to become complacent as a believer.

You weren't born again last night, which is a blessing. You won't fall for the little basic stuff. But the devil knows how to be subtle. The good news, however, is that he is an old dog who doesn't have any new tricks. The tricks are the same over and over again, which is an advantage for us. The biggest difference when you are more mature in your relationship with the Lord, however, is how slick the deceptions can be. So instead of tempting you with that man or woman who sells weed, cusses, fights, and parties all the time, he might tempt you with a "man of God" or "woman of God" you met in the church who seems holy on the surface but is even more of a hot mess than any unsaved person you ever dealt with. This is why we must learn to use the Holy Spirit to help us tell the difference between evil and good. Never get to a place where you think you are too smart, wise, or mature to get got. Learn to listen to the Holy Spirit inside of you, your secret weapon!

READ TODAY: JOHN 16:13

31

DAY 30
I AIN'T GONE HOLD YA.

This phrase has multiple functions. For one, it can be used as a disclaimer/expectation setter. When someone calls you and immediately says, "I ain't gone hold ya..." they are letting you know that they only need a few minutes to say what they have to say. They don't plan to keep you on the phone for very long. The phrase can also be used to signal that a person is ready to hang up the phone. "Well girl, I ain't gone hold ya. I just wanted make sure you knew what was going on with Michelle." It's funny because sometimes people will say this after having already held you for 30+ minutes.

Have you ever felt like you would literally fall over if somebody blew on you? If you are a parent with young kids, I know you know. If you've ever been sick, if you've ever been heartbroken, or if you've ever had a difficult/demanding job, I know you know. During those times, we begin to feel like babies or young children just wanting and needing to be held by someone who loves us and cares. Sadly, as adults in a world with other busy adults, there won't always be someone available to drop everything to support us every time we need it.

Well, be not dismayed. God does love us, and He is willing, ready, and able to hold us. In today's world, adulting can feel like living in a pressure cooker. Rather than explode, I would like to invite you to be held by God, Himself. He can **hold you down** by covering you and by calming the mental storms. And He can **hold you up** to keep you from falling or failing when all you want to do is give up. Let God hold you today. Pray, cry, breathe, and then just surrender the issues to His control. Take comfort in knowing that if God doesn't hold it, it just won't be held. Take your hands off of it now. Let God hold it and you.

READ TODAY: ISAIAH 41:13

DAY 31
AHT! AHT!

So I actually wrote this "Aht! Aht!" devotion for my second book, *God Be Knowin'*. But not many people know about that book, so I'm going to modify and use it here too because it fits. I think we know that "Aht! Aht!" is the sound effect that parents use when trying to quickly warn a child that they need to stop whatever they are doing. I don't know what it is about the sound, but even young babies seem to understand what it means. It's a very urgent sound, because sometimes parents don't have enough time to safely stop and explain their thought processes to a toddler.

If you have the Holy Spirit living inside of you, you may be very well acquainted with "Aht! Aht!" Some people liken the Holy Spirit to having a conscience. Although it's not exactly the same thing, the Holy Spirit acts like a guide and will often hit you with a warning to let you know when you are headed towards trouble. The question becomes, what do you do when you know the Holy Spirit is telling you to chill out? Do you ignore it and continue, or do you go somewhere and saddown? As inconvenient as it may feel to not to get your way all the time, think of the Holy Spirit as that loving parent who doesn't want their child touching a hot stove. We would be wise to listen and obey. God doesn't always take the time to explain to us why we had to stop or change directions quickly. There are some things that we won't fully understand until later. But it's better to learn the lesson by looking back on what you avoided vs learning it by getting burned by your disobedience. Pray today that God would help you to better discern and be obedient to the Holy Spirit's guidance in your life.

READ TODAY: LUKE 6:46

DAY 32
MOVING OUT THE WAY

Have you ever seen a baby that seemed to be developing and hitting certain benchmarks a little faster than other babies at that age? Perhaps they were holding their head up and looking around on day one out of the womb. Perhaps they started rolling over at only two months old. Maybe they began to walk at nine months old. When black people see a baby doing these things, they will almost inevitably respond by saying he or she is, "moving out the way." They mean that this child is moving faster so that they can make room for your next baby to come quickly after. A sleep-deprived parent of a newborn does **not** want to hear this at all!

There's something to be said about moving things out of the way. In life, you will find that certain people, places, things, and mindsets are obstructive. This means that they are blocking your view and therefore, your path. Are there things in your life that need to be moved out of the way so that you can see clearly to run the race of life? The Bible tells us to "lay aside" anything that weighs you down and holds you back, especially sin. Nobody wants to hear this, but sometimes it's simply a mindset that is the sin. Yup, you can literally have a way of thinking that is in and of itself, a sin. You don't have to go out and slap somebody to sin. You can allow anger, bitterness, and violence towards that person to reside in your heart, and that is sinful.

So let's hold ourselves to a higher standard, even mentally. If there is any person, place, thing, or mindset in your life that refuses to develop, refuses to grow, and refuses to mature, perhaps it's time to move it out of the way. Ask the Holy Spirit to reveal what these things may be and the best way to remove them if necessary.

READ TODAY: MATTHEW 5:27-30

DAY 33
WHERE IS HIS HAT?

While we're on the topic of things black folks tend to say to new parents, let's talk about this one. If it's cold outside and you are walking around with a baby, the first question some black folks will ask is, "Where is his hat?" They aren't worried about asking how you're doing or anything cordial like that. They want to know the exact latitude and longitude of the baby's hat and why it isn't on his or her head. Black people of a certain age don't play about cold weather and a hatless baby.

As a young parent, older black folks can be a bit overwhelming at times, but you know...that baby does need a hat. (Maybe I'm becoming older black folks.) A baby can lose body heat through their head and face, so a hat can help comfort your baby and protect them from the harshness of a cold environment.

The Bible speaks about a hat that is just as important for all believers. I'm calling it a hat, but it's really a helmet. The "helmet of salvation" is mentioned as a part of the "whole armor of God" that's found in Ephesians 6. And just like the baby's hat is meant to protect him, so is the helmet of salvation meant to protect us. But what is it really? The helmet of salvation is the protective quality of the **mindset** that we take on when we decide to accept Jesus Christ as our savior. We are to take off old, sinful, and foolish mindsets that cause us harm in the harsh conditions we face in the world. We should then put on the helmet of salvation by adopting the protective mind of Christ. So I ask you the same question. Where is your hat?

READ TODAY: PHILIPPIANS 2:5

DAY 34
THEY GON' SLEEP GOOD TONIGHT.

"Things Black Folks Love To Say About **Your** Child" is still the category. Whenever we see children running around and having a good time, there's this irresistible urge that rises up from the depths of our souls, takes over our vocal cords, and has no choice but to say, "They gon' sleep good tonight." Sorry, not sorry! We can't help it, but you have to admit that it's a great strategy. If you can get the children to use up all of that excess energy, you have a better chance of getting them to go to sleep sooner and for a longer time. They will get good sleep.

I'm concerned that some of you may be expending excess energy during the day and still not getting good sleep at night. Could it be because that excess energy is being used to worry? Could it be that you can't get good sleep because you don't know how to silence the thoughts that crowd your mind all day? If you're like me, you're constantly thinking about tasks that need to be completed and problems that need to be solved.

The Bible tells us not to worry or be anxious about our lives, because it's God's job to take care of us anyway. Also, worrying doesn't even help. We have to stop trying to do God's job for Him. I can't tell you how many times in the past few years that I have said to myself, "Welp! I'm finna put it in the hands of the Lord and take my butt to sleep." You can sleep much more peacefully when you do that. But to be able to do that, you have to truly believe that God has your best interest in mind and that He is **always** working on your behalf in all things. He knows what you need and how to get it to you. Can you believe that? If you can believe that, you can sleep good tonight.

READ TODAY: MATTHEW 6:25-34

DAY 35
YOU HUNGRY?

Parents are humans, which means that sometimes they make mistakes. For some reason, however, most of our parents didn't directly own up to any of the mistakes they made. Let's just say your mom went off on you for breaking her favorite mug. She didn't believe you when you said you didn't break it, but later that evening, she discovers it was your dad who broke it all along. Black parents back in our day didn't come to your room and say, "I apologize." Instead, they'd stick their head in the door and say (with the most gentle voice you've ever heard), "You hungry?" That's it. That's the apology.

It's funny when we think back on it, but hopefully we aren't following in our parents' footsteps on this one. It's okay to admit that you got something wrong and to apologize. Sadly, far too many of us won't humble ourselves enough to do it. The Bible even speaks on the importance of asking forgiveness from the people we have wronged. Matthew 5:25 tells us that if you come to the altar trying to give an offering of some sort, and you remember that you did somebody wrong, just put your offering down at the altar, go fix it with them, and then come back to give your gift. I mean, wow! The Lord doesn't even want your funky lil' offering until you go apologize. That's big.

Use this as your reminder. If you have someone you should apologize to, humble yourself, make the apology, and then leave the rest to God. That person may or may not forgive/accept it, but guess what? That is between them and God. All you can do is your own part. Don't let pride block you from your blessings. Obey God and let Him handle the rest.

READ TODAY: MATTHEW 5:23-24

DAY 36
CHARGE IT TO MY HEAD AND NOT MY HEART.

Whenever black folks are called upon to offer words of gratitude, we must make the all-important decision whether or not to "call names." If we do decide to thank people by name, we are bound to forget someone. In order to avoid hurting the feelings of whoever was forgotten, we give the disclaimer, "If I left anybody out, charge it to my head and not my heart." This means that even though my brain forgot to mention you, my heart is still in the right place.

The Bible tells us that it is better to trust in the Lord with your whole heart than to place confidence in your own intellect. And yet, we often put more confidence in our own limited, biased, emotionally-driven, short-sighted, and easily-influenced brain power than we do in the power of our all-wise, all-knowing Heavenly Father. How foolish! When issues arise in life, do you start by thinking of the best solution, or do you start by praying for the best solution? We are all guilty of this. Yes, God has given us knowledge and intellect, but He does not expect us to use it in the absence of wisdom. And what is the wisest thing you can do in any given situation? Right! Whatever the Lord says!

Sometimes the Lord will guide you to do or say something that doesn't fully make sense to you. If you reject it and go your own way, you will eventually regret that decision. God's way is the best way. God's intellect is the best intellect. If you think that your brain can outthink or out-know His, you are sadly mistaken. So stop charging stuff to your own head, and begin charging it to a heart that truly trusts in the Lord.

READ TODAY: PROVERBS 3:5-6

DAY 37
IF MY MAMA HADN'T PERMED MY HAIR...

Growing up as a black girl in America is a very unique experience, especially when it comes to hair. Back in the 90s, our moms did the best they could to make sure that our hair looked nice and presentable. Sometimes this included a hot comb (see tomorrow's devotion), and sometimes black moms would try to make their jobs easier by relaxing (aka perming) their daughter's hair. Over time, however, we learned more about the potentially damaging effects that perms can have, and many of us began to stray away from them. But there was always that one girl who would say, "Yeah...my hair would've been down my back too if my mama hadn't permed it when I was 8." It's become somewhat of a running joke to now blame any number of shortcomings on the fact that our mama permed our hair. The funniest one I saw was a video on Instagram where a girl was twerking, and a commenter said, "I would've been able to move like that if my mama hadn't permed my hair when I was 12."

That brings me to today's message. What shortcomings do you excuse by placing the blame on others? How long will you blame what your parents did or didn't do for the choices you **continue** to make for yourself? How long will you blame an ex for your current state? At what point will you take accountability, seek God for healing, take authority over it, and go on to be who He has anointed you to be? That's really it. That's really the message. Sometimes I wonder if things would have been different had Adam and Eve taken accountability over their mistake. They chose to blame the next person for their own short-coming, and the rest is history. Let's take charge today. It's not the perm you got 30 years ago. It's the decision you made 30 seconds ago. Amen? Amen.

READ TODAY: GENESIS 3:12-13

DAY 38
HOT COMB

Trigger Warning Today's devotion deals with hot combs. If you have ever had your ear, neck, or scalp burned by a hot comb, you may be entitled to compensation. Well…not really, but wouldn't that be nice? If you're somehow unfamiliar with hot combs, this was a metal comb, usually heated on a stovetop, that allowed black women and girls to straighten their naturally curly/kinky hair, using heat. The results were pretty, but the comb was so hot, that if it ever nicked your skin, it was extremely painful and would sometimes result in a scab.

The issue that many of us black girls had was the gaslighting that took place around hot combs. To calm us down, our moms would tell us that it was just the steam or the hot hair grease we were feeling and that we didn't actually get burned with the hot comb. Well, the scabs that popped up a day later determined…that was a l*e. (I'm still scared to say it. Love you black mamas!)

By now, you're probably wondering what this has to do with the Lord. Well look, the devil is the one that keeps on burning you over and over again. He gaslights you and says, "Oh well…you're not really getting burned. You're fine. Everything is fine." And before you know it, you have a head and heart full of bruises, scabs, and scars because you continue to sit in the devil's chair and listen to his lies. If you think you're going to continue with sin and that it won't have an effect on your mind, body, and spirit, you've got to think again. You're going to get burned. As a matter of fact, you're already getting burned. You've just been deceived into thinking that it's fine. Whatever short-term benefit that your sin seems to have, and no matter how good it looks, it's not worth the lasting effects. Pray and ask God to help you get away from the devil's hot comb chair.

READ TODAY: ROMANS 6:23

DAY 39
HOLD YOUR EAR.

Yesterday we talked about hot comb trauma. Today, I want to bring out another phrase that black moms employed during that process. Having smooth edges was (is) a really important part of completing a black girl's hairstyle. In order to accomplish this, the hot comb had to come extremely close to our skin, and particularly, our ear. When the time came, our moms would tell us to hold our ear down and out of the way to keep it from being burned.

Man. Have you ever been in a situation that made you wish you had never even heard what you heard? Do you ever wish you could return certain details back to the sender? There have been times where certain "tea" was poured that I wish I could just pour right back in the tea pot. Unfortunately, we can't go back and unhear what we've already heard. That's why it's so important to set a healthy boundary when it comes to what we allow to enter our ears. Sure, gossip can be tempting at times, but the Bible says that it can actually have an effect on our souls by increasing our ungodliness. We definitely don't need that!

A sure sign of maturity is when you can stop someone mid-conversation and hold your own ear down and away. All you have to say is, "Hey…I don't even need to know all of that." Your peace does better, and it keeps you from wanting to judge people. It also allows you to continue being your genuine self when you're around them instead of having to play dumb in their presence. And it's not just gossip. Sometimes we need to hold our ears when people want to share all of their own personal business as well. Pray and ask the Holy Spirit to help you to recognize when it's time to listen and when it's time to hold your ear down and away from foolishness.

READ TODAY: 2 TIMOTHY 2:16

DAY 40
IF I COME IN THERE AND FIND IT...

Have you ever told your parents that you couldn't find something that you were looking for? Well our parents were hard working individuals, so they really didn't want to get up and help you look for it. But perhaps they would shout out places that you should go look. "Did you look under your bed?!?" After exhausting all ideas, we'd tell our parents that it's nowhere to be found. They would then sigh and finally get up from their comfortable resting place to come help. On their way, they would often say, "Now if I come in there and find it..." followed by some kind of empty threat.

I don't know what it was/is about "parental" eyes, but as an optometrist, I would love to see the research that explains why a parent can walk into a room and find something instantly when their child has been searching for it for 20 minutes. Honestly, it's embarrassing if you're the child. But for some reason, we just couldn't see it.

It can be this way with our lives as well. There are things about us...things within our hearts, that we miss. Even with all of our soul-searching, there are still things that our Father can come in and find for us. That's why David would sometimes ask God to search his heart. He wanted any of his potentially wicked ways to be found by God and removed from his heart. It's not enough to search your own soul. You're grading your own paper that way. There may be clutter or even a familiarity that prevents you from noticing things that are in plain sight. Don't be afraid to know the truth. Ask God to search your heart and help you to purify it.

READ TODAY: PSALMS139:23-24

DAY 41
YOU SMELL LIKE OUTSIDE.

Can I describe what outside smells like? No. Can you? No. But when someone walks inside, smelling like outside…it's unpleasant. Please don't sit down, don't hold a conversation, and for the love of all that is holy, please don't hug or get near me smelling of "outside." Go get clean, put fresh clothes on, and come back smelling like inside.

As quickly as I can, I'm going to tell you about these three Hebrew boys, Shadrach, Meshach, and Abednego. They were living in Babylon, a nation that didn't worship God. It became law that anyone who refused to bow down and worship the golden statue of King Nebuchadnezzar would be thrown into a fiery furnace to die. The boys refused to bow. They were thrown into the fire, but they did not burn. They walked around in there like it was no problem. A fourth man even appeared in the furnace with them, and witnesses said the fourth man looked like "the son of God." The king was astonished. He called the boys to come out of the fire and proceeded to praise God.

The Bible says that not only were they unharmed, but that they didn't even smell like smoke *insert violent praise*. I just stopped by to tell somebody today who's going through the fire, that a) Jesus is with you in it, b) you won't be burned, and c) you won't even smell like outside! My God Today!

READ TODAY: DANIEL 3:24-30

DAY 42
JUST HUSH AND RIDE.

If your memory serves you correctly, you will probably remember a time when your parents got you ready, put you in the car, and didn't tell you where you were going. This is so hard for a curious child to accept. We ask, "Where are we going? Are we going to the store? Are we going to grandma's house?" Eventually our parents will get tired of our questions and say, "Just hush and ride."

Sometimes in life, we find ourselves having no clue what God is up to or where He is taking us next. Some of us are so used to feeling in control, however, that we don't know how to simply sit back, relax, and accept that God is moving on our behalf. Can you trust Him to drive the vehicle that gets you where He wants you to be? Or are you in the back seat complaining and having an anxiety attack because you don't know what will come next? When we were kids, we trusted that our parents weren't taking us anywhere that would harm us. They didn't have that kind of track record, so we knew they weren't getting ready to leave us on the doorsteps of an orphanage. We have to be the same way with God. His track record indicates that He will neither leave nor forsake us. It also indicates that wherever He is taking us is a **blessing.**

Instead of complaining and going crazy, we should just accept our place in the backseat of God's vehicle. Stretch out, get comfortable, and enjoy the beautiful scenery. The journey can be just as lovely as the destination, but it's all about your mindset. When you whine and complain, you're just telling God that you're not ready for the destination yet. So just hush, ride, and rest in Jesus.

READ TODAY: PSALM 46:10

DAY 43
AS LONG AS YOU'RE UNDER MY ROOF...

There will come a time in the lives of most adolescents where they will want to do things that their parents do not allow. Perhaps you remember being a teenager who didn't feel the need for a curfew. You wanted to hang out all night without restrictions like some of your other friends. But if your parents cared about you, they probably said something along the lines of, "When you're grown, you can do whatever you want. But as long as you're under my roof, you'll obey my rules." You have to admit...it's fair. They are literally working hard to provide you with food clothing, and shelter. Respect isn't too much to ask.

Let's do another quick Bible story. In Mark 2, Jesus was preaching in a house in a city called Capernaum. The house was so packed with people that there was no way to get in. There was one man who was sick with a paralyzing disease. His friends carried him up to the roof, made an opening, and lowered him down to Jesus. When Jesus saw their strong faith, He healed the man, who immediately got up and walked.

I said all that to say, as long as you're under His roof, you have everything you need. If you can get to where Jesus is, you can be healed, delivered, saved, and set free from anything that has you bound. But we're too busy trying to be grown. We want to move out on our own and away from what we were taught. Sure, you have to obey God's principles, but we forget that "under the roof" with Jesus, we find security, love, protection, and provision. Satan and the world will try hard to draw you away from Jesus. They literally hate Him. They even hate hearing His name. So please don't let people (who won't even be there for you when trouble comes) dictate where you choose to live.

READ TODAY: MARK 2:1-5

45

DAY 44
IF YOU CAN HUH, YOU CAN HEAR.

"Huh?" was never the appropriate answer for a black child when responding to an adult. There was something about saying, "huh?" that was downright disrespectful. (And you had to be absolutely crazy to respond with "what?" when they called you.) But one of my favorite black parent (or teacher) clapback phrases was, "If you can huh, you can hear." That's rich! They were saying if you can say, "huh" that means you heard me, so stop acting like you don't know what I said!

I admit that there were a few times when I tried to act like I didn't hear my parents in an effort to stall. Let's just say I was on the verge of getting the bonus rings on Sonic the Hedgehog when my mom called out to me. I might act like I couldn't quite hear what she said, which would buy me a few more seconds to complete the round.

We may have gotten away with that with our parents, but we have to stop trying to get away with that when it comes to God. I'm not going to beat around the bush here. You know good and well you heard Him calling you. Stop acting like you couldn't hear what was said. Stop trying to act like you're so confused and need God to repeat it. You're trying to stall. You're using your fake confusion as an excuse not to obey. Stop playing the games and put down the controller. You know what God is asking you to do. If you're honestly confused, it's not because of God. He is not the author of confusion. So let's stop lying to ourselves and procrastinating. Let's be quick to hear and obey. It's okay to say ouch today. I did!

READ TODAY: MATTHEW 11:15

DAY 45
IF YOU LIKE IT, I LOVE IT.

Have you ever heard a friend saying something that you didn't quite agree with? Perhaps, for one reason or the other, you didn't want to burst their bubble, but at the same time, you didn't want to lie to them. Take for example, a woman who tells you about her new man. She's excited about him, but you can already see the red flags flying high. You might reply with, "Well Sheila, if you like it, I love it!" This is a slick way of saying, "I don't personally like it, but ok. I guess if it makes you happy, then I'm happy for you."

My sister, Alexandria, recently told me that she stopped saying this. Instead, she says, "If **you** like it, **you** love it!" She explained, "Girl, I just remove myself from the equation all together." This is funny but genius at the same time. Alexandria didn't even want it to be suggested that she approves of things that she does not.

When you see things that you know are in opposition to God's word, how do you respond? Do you silently go along with them, or do you let your true feelings be known? There is a time and place for everything. Not everything is your business nor your assignment. And yet, some things are. How do you know the difference? This is why it's so important to have a close relationship with the Holy Spirit. The Holy Spirit can speak to your heart and let you know when it's time to shake your head and keep moving. He can also tell you when it's time to stop and say what you see. We've all had times when we regret what we said or what we didn't say in a situation. Let us ask the Holy Spirit to make us more keenly aware of the difference between a distraction and an assignment.

READ TODAY: PHILIPPIANS 1:9-10

DAY 46
FITTY LEM

"Fitty Lem" or "Fifty Lem" is an official number in the black community. We don't know exactly where it came from, nor do we know exactly how much it is. But for us, it is a valid unit of quantification and/or measurement. Some scholars say that fitty lem is 5,011 units, but that theory has been disputed heavily in several peer-reviewed research journals. If you say a man has fitty lem kids, for example, we don't know exactly how many kids he has. All we know is that he has **a lot.** *Fitty lem means a lot.*

Perhaps you were blessed with a silver spoon in your mouth at birth. That's awesome! But many of us have had to work our way through life. Sometimes we were just thankful to be "getting by." That's cool, but scraping by, living paycheck to paycheck, and just barely making it, is not God's will for your life. We serve a God of abundance. Jesus even said that He came to earth so that we would be able to experience life more abundantly. And that's not just limited to finances. He wants us to experience an abundance of joy, peace, love, health, and wealth in our lifetime. He doesn't just want us to have one or two little blessings. He is the God of increase, overflow, more than enough, and fitty lem!

So let's stop normalizing the lack, and start believing God for the fitty lem. If you're continuing to experience lack in an area, it's your job to search the scriptures and familiarize yourself with the promises as well as the requirements for God's best. His word is the roadmap for abundant living.

READ TODAY: JOHN 10:10

DAY 47
FRIED, DYED, & LAID TO THE SIDE

When I became a teenager, my mom stopped hot combing my hair in the kitchen and would occasionally let me go to the hairdresser instead. Whenever I returned home with my hair looking nicely done, my dad would always say the same line. "Fried, dyed, and laaaaaid to the side!" Now at the time, my hair was clearly neither fried nor dyed, and it may or may not have been laid to the side, but this phrase once served as a compliment in the black community. It meant that you had successfully taken your hair through the process of beautification.

Have you ever considered that perhaps God is taking you through a beautification process? If you've ever been to a beauty salon, you know that the process to beautification can look ugly. At any given shop, you will see women going through various phases of "frying, dying, and laying to the side-ing." During these phases we look a mess, but the process is intentional. At times, the process may even be uncomfortable (anybody ever sat under a dryer for 2 hours?). But when we put ourselves in the hands of a licensed professional, we expect that the results will be worth the process.

I just want to remind you today that God is a licensed professional who knows exactly what He's doing. His process may be uncomfortable, and at times it won't look pretty. But once your sin has been fried, your flesh has been dyed, and your burdens have been laid to the side...you're coming out as pure gold! The results are beautiful. Just continue to be patient and obedient throughout the process, and you will be glad that you did!

READ TODAY: 1 PETER 1:6-7

DAY 48
EDGE UP

I still remember trying to explain what an edge up was to my white homeboys when I was in middle school. I was shocked that they had no idea what I was talking about. It took me so long to explain to them about how the lines needed to be straight and crispy. "Lines? What lines?" It dawned on me that day that most white boys don't get edge ups, they don't need edge ups, and they don't want edge ups. It just wasn't a part of their culture. Edge ups were specifically for us and specifically by us.

Sometimes God will have instructions that apply to everyone, and other times He will give directions that are specifically for you. God knows you better than you know yourself, and He knows that there may be something you need that others don't. One of the saddest things I see among believers is when the Lord gives someone a specific instruction, but they try to impose it on everyone else. No baby, that was for **you**. Youuu can't go to Essence Fest because God knows how you are. I respect that! But now you're on YouTube telling everybody that Essence Fest is of the devil and anyone who attends is going to hell? Come on. I've been to Essence without getting drunk or compromising my witness, and I honestly had one of the best corporate worship experiences of my life when Fred Hammond, John P. Kee, The Clark Sisters, and Kirk Franklin took the mainstage! Does anybody else remember that year?! The year the entire arena sung "Melodies From Heaven" together? Okay, I digress.

Sometimes it's best to focus on our own personal obedience and willingness to follow God's instructions first. If God gives you a message to share with others, it will be filled with love and not just rebuke, condemnation, fear, guilt, and shame. Okay, love you! Bye!

READ TODAY: ROMANS 14:10-14

DAY 49
LORD WILLIN', I'LL SEE (AGE) COME (MONTH).

Have you ever tried to ask a saved, older black person how old they are? They aren't going to simply say, "I'm 81." Nah, that's too easy. They are going to say, "Lord willin', I'll see 82 come November." This is their way of saying that they don't know what the future holds, or even if they will see tomorrow, but if it's the Lord's will, they will be blessed to make it to another birthday.

This is just another reminder that we need to use our time and energy wisely. Honestly, tomorrow isn't promised to anyone, and we must live our daily lives with that understanding. If you knew exactly how much time you had, would you make different choices? My godfather suddenly passed away one morning in 2020 while he was getting ready for work. We were all shocked and saddened by it, but we couldn't really be mad. You see, he truly believed in living every day as if it was his last and without regrets. He spoke often about not holding grudges or remaining angry. He even got on to me once because I was talking about what I would be doing "this time next year." He wasn't against planning, but he wanted to make sure I was living fully for today and not for a day that may never even come.

Think about that. Let's all do our best to be grateful for today. Don't give anyone or any situation the power to steal your joy today. That is a decision that we all must make. Let's not waste our todays being upset about our yesterdays or worried about our tomorrows. God can heal you from your past and He can give you victory over your future. Your assignment is to live in such a way that you can be available to be used by God **today**. Be present.

READ TODAY: JAMES 4:13-15

DAY 50
HE'S GOOD PEOPLE.

If a black person ever describes you as "good people," you have just received an excellent compliment. This is what people say when they are vouching for you to other folks. Let's say, for example, you want to invite a friend to come on a trip or vacation with a larger group that isn't familiar with that friend. You'd say, "Nah. Demarcus is good people. He'd fit right in." Everybody can't be given that compliment.

What does your character say about you when you aren't in the room? I think people underestimate the power of good character. There are certain people in this world who will, for various reasons, may lie and attempt to manipulate others to create a false narrative about your character. The question becomes whether or not it is believable. There are things that have even been said of me by people who were mad that I didn't do what they wanted me to do. Some of those things were immediately laughed at and dismissed because my character spoke up for me. Now I'm far from a perfect person, but I knew that I couldn't go around trying to figure out what lies had been told to whom. I knew I didn't have time to go showing my receipts to people trying to defend myself. All I could do was rely on my character and upon God to speak up on my behalf.

And even if people believe the lies about you, God will reveal the truth in His time. He will let folks know that you are "good people." Your job is to stay obedient and focused on the assignments that He has given to you. Years later, there were people coming to me apologizing for the misconception they had about me and for the lies they believed (meanwhile, I had no idea what they were talking about). It's not always easy, but this is your sign to keep your good character intact and allow God to fight for you.

READ TODAY: PSALM 26:1-3

DAY 51
DON'T THROW A ROCK AND HIDE YOUR HAND.

Have you ever had to deal with a passive-aggressive individual? Oh my goodness! It's so draining. It's like they have something they are trying hard to express or accomplish, but they do it in a way that makes it look like they aren't, which is confusing! They don't have the courage of their convictions. A passive-aggressive person will throw a rock, hit you, and then hide their hands behind their back and act as if they haven't got the faintest idea what you're talking about. There was once a guy that I really liked who liked me too. But he was so passively aggressive that I had to walk away. He was cool, but it wasn't worth the struggle it took to communicate openly and honestly as adults. Sometimes you just need to say and do the stuff with your chest.

There was a young brother in the Bible who saved an entire nation by throwing a rock and refusing to hide his hands. There was a giant named Goliath who continued to taunt and threaten the people of Israel. Everyone was afraid to face him, but when David caught wind of it, he was offended that anyone would dare to defy God and threaten His people. In the end, David killed this giant with a slingshot and a stone. David, although young and inexperienced, was the only one brave enough to take this battle head on.

You see, David wasn't afraid of Goliath. He could stand boldly and confidently before an otherwise intimidating giant, simply because He had already seen what God was capable of doing. He didn't have to mince words or plan a passive-aggressive sneak attack. He used God's track record to stand on, and I encourage you to do the same. When you face conflict in your life, you don't have to manipulate your way into a solution. Stand boldly before it, face it head-on, and watch God give you the victory.

READ TODAY: 1 SAMUEL 17:32-37

DAY 52
IT AIN'T WHAT THEY CALL YOU.
IT'S WHAT YOU ANSWER TO.

Whew chile! A whole word. If you were blessed to grow up with the influence of an older black person in your life, you may have heard this one before. Back in my day, grandparents were a different breed than the ones of today. Many of today's grandparents are still young and living their best lives outside in the streets. Honestly, I don't blame them, but I fear that many of our children are missing out on those golden nuggets of wisdom that we used to get from our older generation. If you came home upset because someone at school called you a mean name, they would often say, "It ain't what they call you. It's what you answer to."

It's so important for us as believers to know who we are in Christ. If you don't know and appreciate your own identity, others will try to make one up for you. I don't know why people do that, but some people feel more comfortable when you can fit into the box that they created for you. And I don't care who it is. If it's not what God says about your life, you don't have to receive it. Don't let anyone pressure or manipulate you into doing or being anything outside of what God has called you to do and be. This applies to things that are either positive or negative. If someone calls you a heaux, and that's not who God called you to be, you don't have to answer to that. But even if someone calls you a doctor, and that's not who God called you to be, you don't have to answer to that either. God has a purpose and plan for your life, and it may or may not be understood by those around you. My prayer for you is that you discover more about your purpose and that you will begin to answer to what **God** calls you.

READ TODAY: 1 JOHN 3:1-3

DAY 53
BLIND IN ONE EYE, CAN'T SEE OUT THE OTHER.

I have no idea where this phrase came from, or why we like to say it like this, but it means exactly what it says. It is referring to a person who has no vision. It might mean actual eyesight, or it might be referring to someone who doesn't have enough foresight or insight to see something that is right in front of them and clear to everyone else.

As an optometrist, I work every day to make sure people can see clearly in the natural realm. One of the most heartbreaking things that I see are babies who are born blind. A close second would be seeing people who were once able to see but have now lost their vision permanently. I can only imagine how God must feel when He sees His children walking around spiritually blinded by sin.

You see, sin gets in the way of a lot. When you have willful, known sin operating freely in your life, it blocks your view to the truth. When sin is blindfolding you, you can't see where you're going, which causes you to stumble along the way. You're blind in one eye and you can't see out of the other. Things that are obvious to everyone else, are obscured and fuzzy for you. If you don't have clarity about certain things going on in your life, ask God to show you if there is sin blocking your view and leading you down a path of self-destruction. If so, ask Him to help you identify it and remove it. The good thing about our spiritual vision is that it can be restored. Your vision loss doesn't have to be permanent with God. Ask Him to help you remove the sinful cataracts from your eyes so you can see your path more clearly.

READ TODAY: 2 CORINTHIANS 4:3-4

DAY 54
BIG MONEY GRIP

Have you ever heard this one? You don't hear it as often now, but my dad used to greet some of his friends this way. He'd say, "What's happening, Big Money Grip?" I'm not 100% sure if this is the origin, but my research reveals that there was a character on the show *Sanford and Son* named Grip Madlock. He was an old buddy of Fred Sanford, who nicknamed him "Big Money" Grip. The term became a way to say that someone has a lot of money, although at times it's used as a sly way to hate on another person's perceived wealth.

There's nothing wrong with being wealthy. As a matter of fact, the Bible tells us that God has given us the power to create wealth. But do you have a big money grip? Are you gripping/clutching your money with a tight fist? It's important to exercise wisdom when it comes to our finances, but I want to caution you against being selfish and greedy. When God gives you a resource, He expects for you to be a good steward over it. A part of that is being a generous giver. When we are blessed, we should seek to be a blessing to others. One of my greatest desires is to be used by God to help meet the needs of His children. I used to think that I'd be a big giver once I got rich. But I abandoned that mindset and decided that I can still operate in that generous spirit, even if it's on a smaller scale for the time being.

When you have a tight grip on your money, you're not only being selfish, but you're also operating in fear. It means that you aren't sure whether God will continue to provide, so you hoard everything you get in anticipation of future lack. Does that sound like faith to you? The Bible says that God gives seed to the sower. In other words, if God knows that He can get things accomplished through your hands, He has no problem putting more into them.

READ TODAY: 1 JOHN 3:17

DAY 55
HOW YOU GET EM IS HOW YOU LOSE EM.

Sadly, there are some women who see nothing wrong with getting involved with a married man. And perhaps it is the married man who initiates the adulterous relationship, but the woman knowingly and willingly agrees to it. Before long, she convinces the man to leave his wife for her. "How you get em is how you lose em," is often a word of caution issued to these women. It means that the same way he cheated on his wife for you is the same way that he will eventually cheat on you with the next one. I've seen it happen.

Mainly, I just want to say today that we've got to stop sowing ugly seeds and expecting a beautiful harvest. It just doesn't work that way. It's not just about relationships. It's about everything in life. Treat others how you would like to be treated. Maintain your integrity. There are certain principles that God set in motion that will remain in place until the end of time. One of those principles is seed time and harvest time. When you sow a seed, you will reap what you sow. You're never going to plant a watermelon seed and harvest a turnip.

Please stop trying to use these underhanded, backdoor means to achieve happiness. Stop trying to scam others to achieve wealth. Stop using good sex to catch a husband/wife. Stop lying about who you are to get someone else to accept you. It may look like it's working temporarily, but if it's built on the wrong foundation, it will eventually crumble. Look to God to supply all of your needs. I know it may look like others are prospering in their wickedness, but you don't want the kind of harvest that they will have to deal with. It's better to be patient and do things God's way. Sow good seeds, be patient, and wait for your good harvest.

READ TODAY: GALATIANS 6:7-9

DAY 56
DO I LOOK LIKE DRIVING MISS DAISY TO YOU?

First of all, *Driving Miss Daisy* is a whole entire movie title, which makes this even more hilarious. Our parents would ask this question whenever they were tired of us asking to be driven around from place to place. We were pretty active as children, but it's much worse now. Kids today have so much going on. It's almost as if chilling at home is a sin now. Being a parent makes me much more grateful for all of the things my folks allowed us to do growing up.

If you're not familiar with the movie, a black man (played by Morgan Freeman) served as the driver for an older white woman after she crashed her car and was no longer fit to drive herself around. He often had to humble himself in order to fulfill his duties as her servant. They eventually formed a close relationship despite their different backgrounds and prejudices.

I brought all of this up to talk about servanthood and humility. In a world where everyone is so concerned about "getting mine," let's not forget how important it is to adopt the mindset of a servant. Jesus set the example for us. He was the King of Kings and Lord of Lords, yet He came in the form of a humble servant. He didn't come to be waited on hand and foot, although He would have been quite justified in doing so. But if **Jesus** came to serve, then why do **you** get in these people's restaurants and treat your waitress like she's some slave who is beneath you? Eww. Humble yourself! I pray that no one reading this ever acts like that.

Hopefully, you know that you're not too good to serve the needs of those around you. It may not be much more than a smile and an encouraging word to someone, but we should always be looking for ways to be used by God in service to the world. That's what makes you great in God's eyes.

READ TODAY: MATTHEW 20:26-29

DAY 57
LIKE WHITE ON RICE

There comes a time when good parents realize that they have to be a little more involved and attentive in the lives of their children. This usually comes after a child has either gotten in some sort of trouble or underperformed academically. A black parent might say, "From now on, I'm gonna be on you like white on rice." This means that they can no longer trust you to do certain things your own, so they will now be vigilant about making sure you are doing exactly what you're supposed to be doing.

Just like a parent who is on their child "like white on rice," God constantly has His eyes on His children as well. You really can't hide anything from Him because He's always there. If that thought bothers you, then you're the problem! When I say that He's always there, does it sadden you to think that you can't get anything over on God or hide things from Him? Honestly, knowing that God is always there with us should be a comforting thought, not a burden.

I'm grateful that we don't have to figure out where God is. I'm grateful that whenever we call Him, He is already right there. There is safety in knowing that God always has His eyes on us. He's on us like white on rice, and that's actually a blessing! The world is a very difficult place at times, and I would hate to have to go through life without Him by my side. Let's take a little time today to thank God for His consistent presence in our lives. Let's do our best to walk upright before Him, knowing that nothing is hidden from His sight.

READ TODAY: PSALMS 139: 7-18

DAY 58
YOU STRAIGHT?

Have you ever been in a situation where you just weren't okay? I know I have. During those times when you're not okay, it can be especially difficult when people expect you to continue functioning at 100%, when you're just not there. Sometimes all we want is for someone to notice that we're not okay and to sincerely inquire about our well-being. When a black person says, "You straight?" they have noticed that something seems a bit off, and they are asking if you are okay.

A little bit of compassion goes a long way. Checking on people goes an even longer way. It's easy to get wrapped up in our own lives and in our own problems, but let this be your reminder today to check on someone. We live in a society where people would rather record a tragedy for social media clout than to step in and actually assist. These days, people will "go live" before they will even dial 9-1-1 on your behalf. Let's not be like that. When people are going through issues, or if you perceive something to be wrong with someone, is your first thought to go and call your friends to spill the tea? If so, that needs to change. If you live long enough, there will come a time when you're going through a "valley experience" yourself. Remember what we learned a couple of days ago? We have to sow those good seeds because eventually it will be time for us to reap that harvest. And it's not as difficult as it sounds. Sometimes it's a simple text message that says, "You ran across my mind today. You straight?"

Pray today and ask the Holy Spirit to remind you of anybody that you are supposed to be checking on. Don't worry about it being awkward. Sometimes we have to get over ourselves and our own discomfort in order to do the will of the Father. If you have love in your heart, share it with someone else.

READ TODAY: PHILIPPIANS 2:4

DAY 59
YOU STRAIGHT.

No, this is not the same devotion as yesterday. Yesterday's devotion was "You Straight?" But today's devotion is "You Straight." Every black person should know that these phrases have two totally different vocal inflections which give them two totally different meanings. When a black person says that you're straight with a period at the end, it means that you are forgiven for whatever offense you may have committed or for whatever accident may have happened. If you stepped on somebody's shoe, for example, and began to apologize profusely, they may relieve your worries by saying, "You straight."

Man, I am so grateful that we have a loving and forgiving God. Some people love to bring up the crazy things you did in your past. Some will even try to make you pay for those mistakes for the rest of your life. They benefit from never letting you forget about what you did. God is the complete opposite. Once you repent (change the way you think), and ask God to forgive you, He does just that. He doesn't even remember them anymore. The only one who wants you in a perpetual state of condemnation, shame, and guilt is Satan.

God said you're straight. That part of it is settled and done. Now it is your job to change your ways to match up with God's ways. You can't go and change the past, but you can take on a new, godly mindset in the present and future. When you pray today, make sure to thank God for His forgiveness. Also, be sure to ask the Holy Spirit to enable you to move on to better.

READ TODAY: HEBREWS 10:17

DAY 60
I CAN'T CALL IT.

When you ask a black person how they are doing, you really don't know what you'll hear next. There is a wide array of possible responses. One such response is, "I can't call it." You may also hear "I can't eem much call it." When somebody says this, it means that they honestly don't know how to answer.

You have to respect someone who admits that they can't call it. We're living in a time where people are obsessed with feeling like they know everything. It takes humility to admit that not only do you not know everything about the world, but you don't even know everything about yourself.

The Bible tells us that the heart is deceitfully wicked and then questions "who can know it?" This means that I can't even call my own heart! That's right. We can be so certain that our heart is right in a situation where it might not be. We can be deceived into thinking our heart is pure towards something when it's really tainted with something that we didn't consider. This is why it's so important to ask God to search our hearts and reveal to us any unclean ways that we couldn't see for ourselves. We may not be able to call it, but God can. Search us Lord and show us anything that we may have missed.

READ TODAY: PSALM 139:23-24

DAY 61
JUST TRYING TO GET LIKE YOU...

I know it doesn't seem like it, but this is another common response you may hear when asking a black person how they are doing. It's a proper black response and also a bit of a compliment. It is translated to mean, "Oh, I've just been busy working hard and trying to get my life together in the same way that yours seems to be."

Whenever someone says, "Just trying to get like you..." in reference to me, I chuckle. I often respond with, "Naw boo...I'm trying to get like **you**!" The truth is, we only see from the outside looking in. We never really know what goes on behind the scenes of another person's life. Social media has made it even easier for us to think that we know more about people than we really do.

If we are going to get like anybody, it should be Jesus. His life here on earth is the best possible example we can follow. When we try to get like Jesus, we go on a journey that helps us discover even more about ourselves. When God created you, He had a plan for you. He designed you in such an amazing way for such an amazing purpose, but life often gets in the way and clouds how we see ourselves. When we learn more about who Jesus really is, we learn more about who we really are. Don't you want to be the highest and best version of yourself? This stressed out, depressed, angry, traumatized, fearful, unhealthy, and unintentional version that you have settled for is not God's plan. The loving, patient, kind, generous, creative, fearless, innovative, healthy, wealthy, and wise version of you is still possible. Look to Jesus.

READ TODAY: HEBREWS 12:2

DAY 62
GOD DON'T LIKE UGLY.

There are several phrases that black people like to quote like scripture even though they are nowhere to be found in the Bible. "God don't like ugly..." is definitely one of them. We often say this when we see a lowdown person get what they have coming to them. Let me tell y'all this quick story.

Earlier this week, my husband called me and was quite upset. Last Monday, he was in the process of emptying his storage unit when his back literally went out on him. His lease was ending, but he only had a few items remaining inside, so he communicated with someone in the office about what happened. This lady assured him that he could come back this week to retrieve the remaining items. The owner, however, had different plans. Since the bill for the new month wasn't paid, he took all of the remaining items to sell off. Included in those items were about 150 copies of my *God Be Knowin'* devotional book. These books had some printing errors, but were mostly okay, so my plan was to eventually find a women's shelter and donate them. The owner said that he looked up the price online and realized that he could sell them and make a good profit. He offered to sell them back to us for $300. My husband was angry at himself for letting it happen and at the man for being lowdown. I wasn't fazed. I told him to let the man have the books. Honestly, I hope they fall into the hands of people whose lives need changing. I'm more worried about the man sowing bad seeds and reaping a bad harvest with God because God doesn't like ugly. That's not written in the Bible, but God does say that vengeance belongs to Him. He will repay those who are ugly to you, so please don't try to get revenge on anyone. It's not worth it. Pray for those people who have sown bad seeds, because they do have a harvest coming, and they must answer to a Father who doesn't play about His kids.

READ TODAY: ROMANS 12:19

DAY 63
IF JOHNNY HAS FOUR APPLES...

Math homework. What a time! I think math homework was the first real introduction to "stress" for many of us as kids. Life was so carefree up until math homework entered the chat. It was not only stressful for us, but for our parents too when we didn't understand the problems. Word problems had some kids and parents in a chokehold. Exhausted black parents would keep repeating the same word problem through gritted teeth, frustrated by their child's lack of understanding. Some would literally begin to yell, "I SAID...IF JOHNNY... HAS...FOUR...APPLES!" Bless their hearts.

Now that I have elementary-aged kids, I get it...especially with the "new math." I don't even understand the new math. Life can be this way sometimes. It can throw stressfully complex problems our way that we feel ill-prepared to handle. Our parents, family, and friends aren't always equipped to help us either. So what do you do as a believer when a difficult problem arises in your life? Do you get frustrated, give up, and accept the failing grade? Are you like our parents, yelling the problem over and over again at different volumes and inflections, even though it doesn't help? This is what we're doing when we spend our time complaining about our problems repeatedly to anyone who will listen.

Instead of focusing so much on the problem, we should focus on the problem-solver. Have you talked more to your friends about the problem than you have talked to God about it? Do you look to memes from social media for wisdom more than you search the word for answers? Do you listen to podcasts from strangers more than you listen to the Holy Spirit? Could the answer to your problem be in plain sight?

READ TODAY: PSALMS 50:15

DAY 64

IF YOU KNEW YOUR SCHOOLWORK AS WELL AS YOU KNOW THEM LYRICS

When black parents and grandparents hear you singing a song, there is this irresistible urge that comes over them. They almost break their ankles running to tell you that if only you spent as much time learning your schoolwork as you have done learning the song lyrics, then you could have all As. They have to say this. I think it's somewhere in the black parenting contract.

As annoying as this was to hear, they weren't lying. So many times in life, we prioritize things that don't matter, while neglecting those things that do. The most important thing should be our faith in God and our daily walk with Him, but so many things come along that distract us from that. We have to be able to recognize distractions when they pop up. I'm going to keep it real. So many people who claim to be followers of Christ haven't taken the time to really learn about their own supposed faith. Some of us have been saved for 20 years and literally know more Biggie lyrics than we do scriptures. That's why these false prophets, preachers, and pastors can come along and lead so many astray with their opinions and false doctrines that have nothing to do with God. We have to study what we say we believe in. Having knowledge of God, His Word, and His promises, is the best protection you can have from Satan and his lies. It's easy to deceive people who don't know much. Let me be a proper black parent and say that if you knew God's word as well as you know what's happening on FB, IG, and TikTok, you could pass these tests, trials, and tribulations of life with flying colors.

READ TODAY: 2 TIMOTHY 2:15

DAY 65
DID YOU GET YOUR LESSON?

If you are a person of a certain age, your parents may have asked you this question. Asking if you have "gotten your lesson" is another way to ask if you have finished all of your homework and/or studied for your tests. My parents didn't say this to me, but my grandparents sure did whenever we went to their house after school. Before we started playing, watching tv, or chilling, they wanted to make sure that we had gotten our lesson first.

So of course, I'm going to ask you the same question today. Did you get your lesson? That last situation that you went through, did you learn the lesson from it? Did you get what you were supposed to get, or are you going to have to keep repeating it until you do? What was that last relationship meant to teach you? What were you supposed to gain from your experiences on that last job? One thing about God is that He's always trying to help us learn and grow. He's very invested in our spiritual maturity, so He sees everything as an opportunity for our development. We must be just as interested and intentional about getting our lessons if we want to be "promoted" to the next "grade level."

Whenever I find myself in a particular situation (and especially if it seems to be a cycle), I'll say, "Okay Lord…what do you want me to get out of this? What are you trying to teach me?" I'm trying to figure out what tools I can take from this season that will help me to do better when I get to my next one. Could you be stuck in an uncomfortable season because you haven't taken the time to learn its lesson? Pray today and ask God to help you get the lessons you need to move onward and upward in His will.

READ TODAY: PROVERBS 4:7

DAY 65
FROM THE GET-GO

I have no idea where we got this phrase from, but I think we all know what the "get-go" is. The get-go is the very beginning of a thing. You may say, for example, "I should have known that relationship wasn't going to work from the get-go, because he eats his grits with sugar instead of salt and butter." Clearly the red flag was there, right?

When people are talking about the get-go, it is often retrospectively. They are looking back on a situation and recounting the things that they should have known or done from the very beginning. Well let me tell you about something that we should all be doing from the very beginning. We should be acknowledging God and asking for His guidance from the get-go. Why do we wait until we are in trouble and desperate before we involve God? Why weren't we interested in His input from the get-go? The Bible tells us that if we acknowledge Him in the beginning of our decision-making process, He will step in and show us which path to take. Instead, we leave Atlanta, headed to California, but won't turn on our GPS until we're lost somewhere in New Jersey! Turn on your GPS or "God Positioning System" from the get-go, and you will reach your destination much sooner and without so much wear and tear on your vehicle. Let's spend some time today praying and asking God to order our steps **before** we even start walking.

READ TODAY: PROVERBS 3:6

DAY 67
IS YOUR DADDY A GLASSMAKER?

Black parents love to ask sarcastic questions. As kids, we would sometimes get so engrossed in a television show, that we'd walk straight up to the TV and stand directly in front of it to make sure that we weren't missing anything. We didn't even think about how we were blocking everybody else's view. Instead of just telling us to move, black parents would yell out, "Is your daddy a glassmaker?" This was a funny way of asking if we thought we were made out of glass and see-through.

Once we remembered that we weren't fully transparent beings made of glass, we'd move out of everyone's way. So let's talk about transparency. I think as a society, we generally like transparent people. They seem to be open, honest, and unashamed about their own imperfections. Naturally, those people are trusted more than those who seem like they are always hiding something. Do you hide your experiences? Do you feel ashamed about the way you used to be or about the things that you may have been through in the past? Perhaps you feel as if no one would relate or that you would be judged too harshly to be transparent. I want to challenge you today to be led by the Holy Spirit when it comes to this, because God might need your transparency to set someone else free from what had you bound. Everything isn't for everyone though, so use wisdom and discernment from the Holy Spirit. If you feel Him tugging at you to be transparent with someone about your journey, please don't ignore it.

READ TODAY: 2 CORINTHIANS 8:21

DAY 68
EVERY WHICH WAY BUT LOOSE...

When a black person says that someone was (or will be) turned "every which way but loose," we are referring to a butt-whooping that they have received or that they have coming. If someone turned you every which way, but did not turn you loose, you lost that fight pretty badly. As a matter of fact, you probably didn't even get a chance to lay a pinky finger on them in your defense.

There was a time in the Bible where an unclean spirit took over a man's body and was turning him every which way but loose. He literally did whatever the unclean spirit made him do including (but not limited to) isolating himself among the tombs, going crazy, crying all the time, and cutting himself with stones. When Jesus showed up on the scene, the unclean spirit freaked out and was afraid because it knew that Jesus had the power to evict it from the man's body and mind.

Let me tell you something, evil/unclean spirits are still at work in people's minds and bodies to this day. Just like the ones in today's scripture, they are still turning some people every which way but loose. People are hurting themselves and others around them because they are allowing Satan's demonic influences into their own spirit. We usually cancel these people and turn them loose ourselves because we feel as if they will never change. Now you may not be able to allow them close proximity to you, and I understand that. But you don't have to turn them loose in the spirit. Jesus is **still** more powerful than any demon could ever be, and they are afraid of His presence. Continue to lift that person in prayer. Continue to call on Jesus and intercede on their behalf. The fight isn't against the individual, but against the spirit that has a hold of them. Always remember that.

READ TODAY: EPHESIANS 6:12

DAY 69
SUITED AND BOOTED

I don't care what they told you, and I don't care what you heard. There is nothing on this planet like a brother who is freshly suited and booted. When we say a man is suited and booted, it means that he is wearing the heck out of a suit and that he has the shoes to match. These days, a properly suited and booted man is hard to come by, so we greatly appreciate whenever we see one.

Today's devotion is just a reminder that as believers, we all need to be properly suited and booted for this thing we call life. The Bible lays out several elements of our "suit" that we should be sure to include if we want to be prepared for success. Ephesians chapter 6 advises us to put on the "whole armor of God" so that we can protect ourselves from the foolishness that Satan tries daily. No, you can't run to the store to find this suit of armor. These are spiritual garments such as truth, righteousness, peace, faith, salvation, and prayer. Look at these closely.

People are often afraid of **truth,** even though the Bible tells us that truth protects us. Don't let the devil deceive you into thinking a lie is safer than the truth. These days, **righteousness** is vilified, and evil is glorified. It sometimes seems safer to go the way of the majority even when it's not right…another trick from Satan. Lack of **peace** is becoming normalized and marketed as everyone simply having anxiety. We don't *all* have an anxiety disorder, some of us just haven't submitted to the Prince of Peace. Your **faith, salvation,** and **prayers** are looked down upon and called delusion. Don't you see it? Satan is trying to trick you into believing you don't need any of God's armor of protection. Don't fall for it. Stay suited and stay booted!

READ TODAY: EPHESIANS 6:11-18

DAY 70
SOMEBODY DONE TOLD YOU WRONG.

"Somebody done told you wrong" is an expression in the African- American vernacular that you can't help but love. It's a funny way of telling someone that they are confused about a matter. If someone says, for instance, "I thought you were going to give me a discount because we went to high school together…" you might respond with, "Naw baby! Somebody done told you wrong! Pay me what I charge just like you would pay anybody else."

I thank God for growing up with encouraging voices and influences in my life. But what happens when a child, teen, or young adult has been indoctrinated with stinkin' thinkin'? These are thoughts, ideas, values, and principles that are simply wrong. I heard someone say (about their own son and in front of him), "He's like me. I wasn't good in school. He's going to end up doing something with his hands." The boy was only 8 years old at the time. Do you see the problem? Those kinds of words seem casual but can set up a mindset in a child that he will not ever be good in school or with his brain, and that his future is limited to manual labor only. Someone had told the father that when he was a boy, and he accepted it at face value and went on to tell it to his son. It never dawned upon this brother that perhaps someone had told him wrong.

Perhaps it was easier for someone to limit you or put you in a box than to work with you and get you the help you need in an area where you struggled. Maybe it was a parent, teacher, family member, church member, or even a pastor who told you wrong about yourself and your potential. I want you to think back today and reject anything that was ever told to you that God did not say. Forgive those people and ask God to tell you what is **right** and true about yourself.

READ TODAY: ROMANS 12:2

72

DAY 71
SENIOR SAINTS

I know I say this in every book, but umm…today is my birthday! Now you may be wondering why this page is titled "Senior Saints." If you've ever been to a black church, you know this is what we call the older men and women within the membership. At the time of this writing, I'm 38 years old. To some that's old, and to others it's young. I injured my shoulder about two months ago because I…get this…made a sharp right turn in my car. That's it. That's all. Traffic was approaching swiftly from the left, so I had to make a quick right turn and my shoulder has been hurting for two straight months. I have an appointment to see if it's my rotator cuff (editors update: it was indeed my rotator cuff). Chiiiile!! It's so ghetto!

Aging can be difficult. My grandfather (my favorite guy) is currently 94 years old. He said, "I don't mind getting old. It's just inconvenient." LISTENNN! But just because we are all getting older physically doesn't automatically mean that we are growing and maturing spiritually. You would think that age and wisdom go hand and hand, but that isn't always the case. Have you ever seen an "old girl" or an "old boy"? They are aging physically but still operating like a child. They never put away the childish things.

That's why I want to encourage you today. Even as our bodies go through this ghetto aging journey, our spirits can be renewed, refreshed, and revitalized like a fountain of youth. But it takes an intentional decision to stop caring about the petty, superficial, unnecessary things that mattered so much to us at one point in time. Move onward and upward in your spiritual journey. So the next time you feel some random ache or pain, let that be your reminder to put away childish things. Happy birthday to me! (Editor's Update: My grandfather has since passed away. He gave me a birthday card with money in it every year of my life. He arranged my last card from his hospital bed! Keep me lifted in prayer today!)

READ TODAY: 2 CORINTHIANS 4:16

DAY 72
A1 FROM DAY 1

I think about how challenging it must be to have English as a second language in the black community, because we just come up with all kinds of stuff. If you say that someone is your A1 from day 1, it means that you and that person have been the best of friends for a long time, maybe even since the first day of kindergarten. If someone has earned the title of A1FD1, it means that their loyalty has been proven and that they have been a consistently positive and dependable figure in your life.

I think we should all take some time to appreciate the original A1FD1, and that A stands for Alpha. He has been there from the beginning. He knew you before you knew yourself. As a matter of fact, He **still** knows you better than you know yourself! And as wonderful as it is to have a best friend, I can guarantee you that even your best friend can never be as much of a friend to you as God is. Friends are great, but if you've ever been up crying alone at 3am, you already know that there are times when the only one able and available to help you is Jesus.

Let's take some time to meditate on that today. Express your gratitude to God and thank Him for being your A1FD1. Honestly, He was our A1 before we ever even had a day 1. Before we ever took one breath, God was already working things out on our behalf. I love God. I hope you do too. Have a blessed day.

READ TODAY: REVELATION 1:8

DAY 73
IF "IF" WAS A FIFTH, WE'D ALL BE DRUNK.

In this common phrase, "a fifth" is referring to a fifth of liquor. When someone says this, they are relaying the idea that anything you say that starts with the word "if" is not fully reliable. "If I get this job I applied for, I can pay you back in a few weeks." Oh okay…if "if" was a fifth. It is the black equivalent of the saying, "If ifs and buts were candies and nuts, we'd all have a Merry Christmas."

The word "if" is often used to introduce something called a conditional clause. God uses several conditional clauses in the Bible when He issues potential promises for us. There are certain promises where God tells us what He will do **if** we do our part. I think that's a huge problem for many believers. They hear about the promises, get excited about them, and ignore the requirements that came with them. Sometimes this leads to disappointment with God and sometimes it leads to anger. We feel that we are entitled to certain promises and blessings simply because we believe or because we pray. But when God lays out specific instructions and we choose to ignore them, why are we mad?

There's one promise in the Bible that says if you are willing and obedient, you will eat the good of the land. Do you want the best God has to offer, but without the pesky obedience? Do you obey out of obligation, guilt, or fear, yet you don't have a truly willing heart? If that's the case, don't be surprised if you're having to eat some unrecognizable meat on a stick from the gas station when God has promised you a five-star restaurant. I challenge you today to study and learn more about God's promises **and** His requirements for them.

READ TODAY: ISAIAH 1:19

DAY 74
IF "IF" WAS A FIFTH, WE'D ALL BE DRUNK (2).

No, I am not having a senior moment. Today is a follow up of yesterday's message. We talked about conditional clauses and how God uses them in His promises to us. Today, however, I want to talk to you briefly about anxiety and fear.

Have you ever talked yourself out of something because you didn't know all the details? There were a lot of "what ifs," and that made you uncomfortable. Perhaps it was even paralyzing. Some of you are probably reading this book right now thinking, "Shoot, I coulda wrote this. I shoulda wrote this." Sometimes we talk ourselves out of being obedient to God because we are so busy thinking about things that are nothing more than remote possibilities. We let those "ifs" scare us into what is honestly disobedience and rebellion to God's clear instructions. Here are some "ifs" that I had to get over. What if they don't like the book? What if it's not deep enough for the super-spiritual people? What if it's too deep for the ratchet people? What if I spend all this time working on a book and nobody even buys it? What if people get mad at me because a message stepped on their toes? What if people decide to cancel me for being a follower of Christ? What if there's a typo and they go online and give me a terrible review? What if my jokes aren't really funny? What if they don't get my humor?

I challenge you to think back about the things that God gave you a dream, vision, or instructions to do. Instead of thinking about the bad ifs, think about the good ones. What if somebody is saved? What if somebody is healed? What if somebody is set free from bondage? What if somebody is blessed? What if somebody's life is changed?

READ TODAY: MARK 9:23

DAY 75
TELL ME WHY...

"Tell me why..." is a story-telling device in the black community. I'm guilty of using this phrase to open a story when I'm talking to my husband or best friend. "Tell me why my 1:00 patient decided to show up an hour late and got mad because she had to re-schedule?! And tell me why she cussed out the receptionist, stormed out the door, and called back 15 minutes later with an attitude, trying to reschedule it?! But how about my manger told her that we can no longer see her but will gladly send her records to a new provider?! The end!"

Of course when we are telling the story, we don't really think our listener will be able to tell us why. However, when it comes to life, there are things...confusing things... that we don't understand, and we just wish God would tell us why they happened the way they did. Out of all people, why were **you** the one to lose a parent at a young age? Out of all your friends who were sexually active, why were **you** the one to get pregnant or get an STD? Why were **you** the one to be let go from that job? Out of all your friends who got married around the same time, why were **you** the one who got fooled by a narcissist? Why are **you** the one getting a divorce? Why did **you** get the diagnosis?

Listen, there is nothing wrong with asking God to tell you why a thing occurred. Shoot...I ask God all the time why my stomach won't get flat. You just have to understand that He may or may not reveal it to you in the timing that you want. But when we really think about it, He's already revealed it to a degree. When He said that all things work together for our good, He lowkey told us why. We just have to wholeheartedly trust and believe that even our hardships will be used by God to bless us. We'll understand it better as we go.

READ TODAY: ROMANS 8:28

DAY 76
ALL THEM BOOK SMARTS AND NO COMMON SENSE

This is really a diss. Have you ever met someone who had all kinds of degrees, but didn't seem smart at all? It seems impossible, but I can assure you, it's not. I've seen people who were on the doctorate level, making some of the most ridiculous life decisions that were clearly made in the absence of common sense. Shoot...I've BEEN people on the doctorate level, making some of the most ridiculous life decisions in the absence of common sense.

I want to talk about how important it is to have sense along with your knowledge. If you've been reading my devotional books, you know that I've never been trained as a writer, and I've never been trained to be any kind of spiritual authority. I don't claim to be an expert in either. I'm just a girl from Alabama who decided to listen to God and obey. I've never been to a seminary or a school of theology. I have nothing against them, but that has not been my path. I've met people however, who have book smarts when it comes to God, the Bible, Hebrew, Greek, and all the rest, but there is no spiritual sense when it comes to a personal relationship with a loving Father. There are people who are so wrapped up in proving the existence of God from a scientific or historic perspective but have never taken time to sense His presence in their own lives.

Knowledge is needed, but the Bible warns us that it can make people "puffed up." Their head is so filled with what they know that they look down on others who don't know as much as they do. My prayer is that as you continue to grow in grace and in the knowledge of our Lord, that you will have much more than book smarts. I pray that you will sense God working in your life, and that your soul will also prosper.

READ TODAY: 1 CORINTHIANS 8:1-3

DAY 77
STREET SENSE

Have you ever met a person who may not have had a lot of education, but they had a whole lot of street sense? These are people who may not be able to help you fill out your tax forms, but they know how to make a dollar out of fifteen cents. They may not know anything about the stock market, but they can negotiate a deal with the salesman and save you thousands on the purchase of your automobile.

A lot of people think that just because we are followers of Christ, that we are these naïve, delusional creatures who are easy to get over on. Some people will mistake your kindness for weakness and will try to take advantage of the fact that you live your life with a standard. They know that we are called to be givers, so they will use that to try and suck you dry. They know that we are called to be humble, so they will try to walk all over you to get their way. They know that we are called to "turn the other cheek," so they will slap you in the face and expect you to be cool with it.

This weak and foolish image of us is in total contradiction to the example Jesus set for us. Yes, we are supposed to be loving, kind, and caring. But we are also meant to be wise and keep our head on a swivel. The Bible calls it "walking circumspectly." This means that as we walk or move forward, we should be looking around in a 360° circle to determine who/what could cause us harm or distract us from our destination. If you ever study how Jesus moved throughout the Bible, you will see that He was a long way from being weak. He got people together as needed. Today, I just want to remind you to be on the lookout for people who seek to take advantage of your status as a believer for their own personal gain.

READ TODAY: MATTHEW 10:16

DAY 78
I **KNOW** THAT'S NOT **MY** CHILD
IN HERE MAKING ALL THAT NOISE.

When you were a kid, did you ever go somewhere with your folks where things got a little out of control playing with the other children? Perhaps you went with your mom to her best friend's house. The grown folks stayed in the living room talking while the kids went to another room to play. But of course, some kids just don't know how to play without screaming and hollering. That's when you would hear your mom (or another mom) walking towards you and saying… "Oh I **know** that's not **my** child in here making all that noise."

The implication here (especially with the emphasis and inflection on "know" and "my") is that this parent expects their child to know better. They know good and well it better be somebody else's child screaming and hollering, even though it sounds just like my child's voice.

I think that's how God is with us sometimes too. We get ourselves into a difficult situation in life, and we allow our circumstances to make us lose our cool. Instead of remaining calm, we are losing it. We are fussing, fighting, crying, arguing, and carrying on with others because of our frustration or nervousness about a stressful situation. I imagine God saying, "Oh…I just **KNOW** that's not **MY** child down there making all that noise." You see, when we have God fighting for us, we should have a calmness that comes as a result of our confidence in Him. If I'm making a bunch of noise over my circumstance, it's a sure sign that I'm not trusting God like I should. Be quiet, be calm, and be **still** because God **is still** sitting on His throne, and He has all power in His hand.

READ TODAY: PSALM 46:10

DAY 79
...AND PEOPLE IN HELL WANT ICE WATER.

This stinging phrase is often used as a reply after someone has expressed a desire for something that you have absolutely no interest in providing for them. Someone might say, for example, "I want a man who makes over five million dollars a year to take care of me, pay all my bills, take me on trips, and require nothing from me in return." Someone listening might reply, "...and people in hell want ice water."

I'm a little worried that we are spoiled brats. What happens when we desire something that we simply cannot have? I'm a little worried that we don't know how to process and respond when the answer is no. Specifically, I'm talking about when our flesh gets told no. Do we try to pacify our carnal desires like we would a baby, simply because our flesh won't stop crying, screaming, and demanding to get its way? Do we take God's "no" and try to find ways to work around it? That is not a good idea, and I will use relationships for example. Have you ever been in a situation where you wanted to be with someone so badly, but God's answer was clearly no? If you powered ahead anyway, or even if you allowed that person to linger in your life, you eventually lived to regret it. You end up wishing you had never met that person or that you had just yielded to God's directions.

As followers of Christ, we are called to crucify our flesh every single day. This means that we have to be intentional about identifying the desires of the flesh that are in opposition to the spirit of God living within us. We must tell the flesh no **every-single-day.** The next time your flesh tries to tell you it wants something it shouldn't have, tell it that people in hell want ice water...and keep it moving!

READ TODAY: GALATIANS 5:24

DAY 80
WHAT DON'T COME OUT IN THE WASH,
COMES OUT IN THE RINSE.

This saying is pretty country. So if you're from the city, it's possible that you haven't heard it. I learned it only recently from my husband. But it's referring to people's secrets being exposed. If it (the secret) doesn't come out in the wash (the beginning), it will come out in the rinse (the end). It's such a clever way of putting it.

If you follow celebrity news, you have seen that there have been a lot of secrets coming out lately. Allegations are swirling about some of the most revered public figures, and people have proof about terrible things that happened 10, 20, and even 30 years prior. Some of these allegations were rumored but never confirmed, and others are shocking things that we never would have expected.

I said all of that to say, please be careful. If you feel the need to hide something, do you really need to be doing it? Consider the fact that things don't stay hidden forever. Just because your secret is well-hidden, this doesn't mean that it's okay. We've heard a million times that what's done in the dark will eventually come to the light. So many people that we look up to are facing civil charges, criminal charges, jail time, and social cancellation for things that they never thought would come out.

No, you may not be able to undo things that you've done in your past, but you can pray and ask God for forgiveness and mercy for those things. And most importantly, do not continue in them just because you feel you are getting away. Ask God to cleanse you from all unrighteousness.

READ TODAY: ECCLESIASTES 12:14

DAY 81
WHAT DON'T COME OUT IN THE RINSE, COMES OUT IN THE WASH (2).

So yesterday, when we talked about this same topic, it dawned on me that it doesn't only apply to things that are sinful. There are two sides to every coin, so I wanted to give you the other side of this one today. If it doesn't come out in the wash (the beginning), it will come out in the rinse (the end).

There are many of you who are secretly doing things that will eventually come out. Some of you have been praying in secret, and I believe the manifestation of your prayers will eventually come to the light. Some of you have been fasting and cleansing your spirit in private, but I know the results are coming for you. Some of you have been giving and sowing into others in secret. You're not doing it for clout or for any kind of recognition, but I do believe that there is a harvest coming for your labor.

Listen, many of you are doing the right things. However, it can be discouraging at times because no one seems to notice, care, or appreciate how hard you work. If you stopped doing what you're doing, so many things would fall apart in so many places, yet there are those who have the luxury of taking it all for granted. I just wanted to send you some encouragement today. God sees what you're doing when you think nobody is watching. He sees the hard work, blood, sweat, and tears that it costs for you to do what you are called to do. Do not give up. Do not get weary. Do not faint. You may never get a "thank you" from the people you blessed, but God is going to reward you for your faithfulness in due time.

READ TODAY: MATTHEW 6:6

DAY 82
EAT YOU OUT OF HOUSE AND HOME

This phrase is usually reserved for ravenous teenagers who seem to eat nonstop when they are at home. If someone is eating you out of house and home, it means that feeding them has become so expensive that it's going to land you in the poor house.

There is a story in the Bible where God commanded his prophet, Elijah, to visit a widow woman during the time of a drought, which had resulted in a famine. He told Elijah to go down to Zarephath where he would find this widow, whom God had instructed to feed him. Elijah asked the widow for some water and then for some bread. She told Elijah that she didn't have any bread. All she had was a handful of flour and a little oil. She had planned to make one last loaf of bread for herself and her son to eat before they died of starvation.

Elijah told her not to be afraid, but to make the bread and to feed him with it first. To many of us, this would be preposterous and pretentious. He was going to eat her out of house and home. But Elijah promised that if she would do this, her jar of flour and jug of oil would continue to be replenished every day until the drought was over. She followed the prophet's instructions, and God did just as He said He would. Her family was saved.

All I want to say today is that if you take care of God's business, He will take care of yours. Stop ignoring that assignment. Stop ignoring His instructions. Stop ignoring His call on your life. You're trying to take care of yourself and struggling to make it, when God is simply asking you to trust Him enough to be obedient even in the midst of a difficult, dry season.

READ TODAY: 1 KINGS 17:12-16

DAY 83
TILL THE WHEELS FALL OFF

If someone says they plan to do something till the wheels fall off, it means that they are going to stick with it until the bitter end. My first car was a Dodge Intrepid. I drove it for many years. I wasn't interested in showing off or having a car note, so my plan was to drive it until the wheels fell off. Well those "wheels" just so happened to be a transmission repair that would have cost more than I paid for the vehicle, but you get my point.

You may be familiar with a time in the Bible where Moses was trying to help free the children of Israel from Pharoah's Egyptian slavery. I guess they must have been making a lot of money for Pharoah, because he did not have any intentions of letting those people go. After a series of plagues, Pharoah finally agreed and let the Israelites flee from Egypt. Not long after they left, he changed his mind yet again, and sent his Egyptian army to chase after them and bring them back to slavery. The children of Israel had fled all the way to the sea, where they realized they had no way to cross. God used Moses to literally split the Red Sea, allowing them to cross on dry land. The Egyptians had horses and chariots and were hot on their trail. Once all the children of Israel had crossed to the other side, the waters went back to their normal position, and the Egyptian soldiers who were trying cross over behind them on chariots, found their wheels falling off. They drowned in the Red Sea.

All I want you to know today is that you can be free from whatever has you bound. It may seem like that thing is going to plague your life forever, but it does have an expiration date. When you keep following God's instructions, He will provide a way of escape, and your enemy's wheels will fall off. They/it can't go where you're going.

READ TODAY: EXODUS 14:22-28

DAY 84
DON'T LET THE DOORKNOB HIT YA
WHERE THE GOOD LORD SPLIT YA.

This is a common phrase that black people will use when they want you to know that you are more than welcome to leave their life or space. I imagine one of those swinging screen doors at my grandmother's house. You could hardly get out of it before it was swinging back on you and threatening to knock you down. Perhaps this saying is really a threat. Maybe they are warning you that they will be closing the door so fast behind you that it may hit you on the behind.

I think we have to be careful about trying to maintain certain friendships and relationships past their expiration dates. Sometimes people even threaten to leave on their own, and we convince them that they should stay. Sometimes we are so afraid of feeling rejected or of being alone, that we settle for situations that are truly detrimental to our minds, bodies, and spirits. Do you ever find yourself jumping through certain hoops to perform for people in order to get them to stay and be satisfied with you? I want you to know that there are certain people who you can literally die on the cross for, and they will still reject you (ask Jesus), because they are honestly not even ordained for you.

There is a time for everything. Please do not be afraid to let things or people go who need to go. I don't care if you have known them since the first grade. If their season in your life is clearly over, do not feel guilted into allowing them to stay. And do not let fear of the unknown, cause you to beg, plead, and perform to keep something or someone that does not want or need to be kept. Pray and ask God to give you wisdom and discernment on when you're meant to stay and fight and when you're meant to let that screen door swing and knock them clear into the bushes.

READ TODAY: 2 CORINTHIANS 5:17

DAY 85
BROKE YOUR PLATE AND BENT YOUR SPOON

Back in my day, kids were expected to have a plan after high school. They were expected to graduate and either go to college, go to the military, go to trade school, or get a job with the intention of being able to soon afford your own place to stay. Things have changed now, and society has changed a lot. The world seems to be a bit crazier than it was, so parents and kids alike seem pretty comfortable with the kids just...staying home and not going out into the world. My first trip home from college, my dad joked that they had broken my plate and bent my spoon. I could tell he had been waiting to use that little line.

A broken plate and a bent spoon is another way of saying "You are officially not my responsibility anymore." I'm sure this is a very liberating moment for parents who have been sacrificing to raise children for 18 years. When we left home as young adults, it was our ambition never to need to return to the custody/care of our parents who would surely treat us like children again.

I'm happy to announce that God is the opposite way! You may have turned your back and walked away from Him, but He never broke your plate, nor did He bend your spoon. Sometimes we allow the temptations of life to carry us away from God. We go the opposite direction of where He is leading, and that causes us distance. But I'm grateful that God, our Father, is willing to forgive us for our sins and cleanse us from our unrighteousness. He allows us to return to our proper place in Him. Do not ever be ashamed to be a child returning home to our loving Father. There is still room for you to eat at His table. Your plate is right there where you left it, and so is your spoon.

READ TODAY: LUKE 15:21-24

DAY 86
TALKING BACK

I think we all know what talking back is. As children, when our parents said something to us, particularly something of a disciplinary nature, we were not to make any reply other than, "yes ma'am" or "yes sir". Anything else could be deemed as "talking back," which was highly disrespectful and could even earn you a whooping. Society has changed now, and many of the parents have adopted a gentler, more lenient parenting style that allows children to talk back and express their stance on whatever they choose. This works for some kids, but then there are other cases where you find a 5-year-old literally yelling and arguing back and forth with their parents in the store like a grown man or woman.

When you pray, do you allow time for talking back? Do you allow time for God to talk back to you concerning the things that you just prayed about? Or do you simply tell God what you want and need and then hop up and carry on about your day? I am guilty of this myself. Sometimes we need to slow ourselves down and take a moment of quietness following prayer to see if we can discern God's voice or His instructions. Prayer shouldn't be a one-sided speech we make to God without allowing His voice to be heard if He chooses to speak.

My challenge to you today is to pray and then silence yourself. Be still and listen to see if you can hear or feel God speaking to your heart. There are things you may be confused about that perhaps He wants to clarify. There may be instructions that He wants to give to steer you in the direction of your breakthrough. The Holy Spirit may want to teach you something or reveal something to you that you needed to see. Talk to God in prayer, bring all your burdens to Him, and allow Him a moment to talk back.

READ TODAY: JEREMIAH 33:3

DAY 87
SLAP THE TASTE OUT YA MOUTH

Has anyone ever threatened to slap the taste out of your mouth? I hope not, because that seems pretty harsh. I mean…how hard do you really have to slap someone to where their taste buds literally just clock out of work? I don't want to ever find out.

You know what's crazy? Have you ever heard of something in the Bible called a "reprobate mind"? This is a state of being where a person has rebelled against God so long and so much that He finally says, "Okay, Imma let you have it fam." It's a state where people are so committed to doing evil or wrong, that God doesn't even allow the Holy Spirit to convict them of their wrongdoings anymore. It's a very unfortunate state because that person doesn't even feel bad or remorseful for the ungodly things they are doing.

It's almost as if their union with Satan has slapped the very taste out of their mouths. Their senses are now dulled to the things of God, and I hate that for them. However, it's what they wanted. So I just want to caution you about continuing on in willful, known sin in your life. If you know that it's wrong but decide that it's okay for you, you are numbing yourself to evil. That is so dangerous, because you don't know just how far down that road the devil plans to take you. I can guarantee you it's farther away than you thought. Don't let Satan slap the appetite for God and for His righteousness out of your mouth.

READ TODAY: PSALM 34:8

DAY 88
RIDIN' DIRTY

I know this was a song released in the early 2000s, but back then I was too green to know what they were talking about. It was just a catchy tune. It wasn't until years later that I learned the real meaning. Apparently, when someone says that they are ridin' dirty, it means that they are operating a motor vehicle without the proper legal documentation to do so. They are either driving with no license, an expired tag, or no insurance. Oh, and the car might be stolen all together. Ridin' dirty is pretty brave. I would be too scared of getting pulled over.

Well there was one guy in the Bible who was ridin' really dirty and ended up getting pulled over by God. His name was Saul, and he was a man who spent his days persecuting (aka trolling) Christians. He was headed down the Damascus Road, literally on his way to capture and persecute more Christians. (He's always depicted as riding on a horse, but it's funny because the Bible never actually says that.) Suddenly a bright light shined on him from heaven. He fell down and heard God's voice saying, "Saul, Saul, why are you persecuting me?" The light was so bright that it blinded him for three days. God sent one of His disciples to speak to Saul and restore his vision. He instantly believed and began preaching Christ and bringing glory to God.

The moral of today's story is that no matter how dirty you may be riding in your life, God can turn it around for you. He can take you and show Himself to you in such a mighty way that you can't help but believe in Him. He can still use you even after the mistakes have been made. Don't allow anybody to make you think that your life is too dirty for God's help. Saul's name was changed to Paul, and he went on to be the most impactful minister of the gospel to this day.

READ TODAY: ACTS 9:1-6

DAY 89
SLOW YA ROLL

"Slow ya roll" is our spiced-up way of telling someone to slow down or calm down. If I say, for instance, that I'm getting ready to go run some errands, and I see my daughter putting on her shoes and heading to jump in the car, I might say… "Slow ya roll lil' baby…I didn't say you could come with me."

Today, I want to talk to you about slowing the rolling motion of your very own tongue. Have you ever said something so quickly without thinking that you wish you could take back? Once your tongue lets something out, it's out. The Bible speaks several times about our tongues. In the book of James, we are taught the importance of having a well-controlled, well-disciplined tongue.

One of the wisest pieces of practical life advice found in the Bible is where it tells us to be swift to hear and slow to speak. It's basically telling us to slow the roll of our tongue and speed up our ability to listen to someone else. I'm still working on this. I've got to do a better job of allowing people to get their thoughts all the way out so that I get a full picture of what is being said. Sometimes I want to stop people when they are saying something wrong or false, but being slow to speak sometimes means letting them get it all out so you can know what they **really** think about you or about a situation. This enables you to move accordingly and with wisdom. I'm not so good at this yet, but perhaps practice makes perfect. Let's all try to do a better job of being better listeners with a tongue that rolls out a little more slowly.

READ TODAY: JAMES 1:19

DAY 90
TELL THE TRUTH, SHAME THE DEVIL.

If I didn't know any better, I'd think that this saying came straight from the Bible based on how much black folks like to quote it. Sometimes you'll even hear messy people using it as a means to encourage someone to spill the tea. If Person A hesitantly says, "Well...I don't know if I should put his business in the street like that." Person B may encourage them to tell it by saying, "Tell the truth, shame the devil!"

Aside from being used by messy people to get juicy details, this statement is actually pretty great. Telling the truth really does shame the devil. The Bible tells us that truth makes us free. If truth is something that makes us free, then using my extra fancy deductive reasoning skills, I can deduce that lies enslave or shackle us to something so that we become bound to it. Sadly, so many people are held captive every single day by lies either coming from someone else or from themselves.

And do you know what else? The Bible says that God has not given us a spirit of fear. That means that if you have a spirit of fear operating in your life, it was given to you by Satan. Let's deduce again. If Satan is the "*Father* of Lies," then the child being reproduced must be fear, and fear is what keeps us bound. So boom...we're back at the beginning. When we operate in a spirit of truth, we kill the fear, set ourselves free, and bring shame to the devil because he is now exposed as the slimy, bucktooth, jack-legged fraud that he really is. How shameful! I challenge you today to think about where fear is operating in your life. Find the lie that is at the root of said fear and pluck it up with the truth of God's word and His promises to you!

READ TODAY: JOHN 8:32

DAY 91
WHO GOT THE BODY?

In America, we typically observe and celebrate the death, burial, resurrection, and ascension of Christ around springtime. We celebrate a funeral that got cancelled when Jesus got up from the grave. So I've decided to do a series of devotions based on things black folks like to say when someone "transitions." I have no idea why, but one of the first questions black people have is, "Who got the body?" They are asking which funeral home is being used for the final arrangements.

You've been reading with me long enough now to know that this is usually where I start asking you the questions. So…who got your body? I know you are saying that your heart and mind belongs to the Lord, but who's got your body? Does what you do with your body match up with what you proclaim to believe in your spirit? Or is there a contradiction there? Do you believe in God up to the point where you have to tell your flesh no?

We are called to reverence and respect our own bodies because they are supposed to be a place where the Holy Spirit can dwell and operate. If we are to house such a precious guest as the Holy Spirit, we should "fix up the place" by allowing God to be Lord over every part of us, even our bodies.

READ TODAY: 1 CORINTHIANS 6:19-20

DAY 92
GONE TOO SOON

When Betty White passed a few days shy of her 100th Birthday, many of us jokingly said that she was "gone too soon." We really wanted Betty to see 100. But we laughed at the irony, because this phrase is normally used by black folks when someone passes away at a relatively young age.

When we remark that a person is gone too soon, we are really just saying that they are gone too soon for our liking. Because the truth is, we have absolutely no way of knowing if someone left this earth at their God-appointed time or before. Tomorrow truly isn't promised to anyone. That's why it's so important to let go of any petty grudges and offenses that we hold against others in our hearts. That bitterness turns into an intense, stinging, sense of grief when that person passes away with issues being unresolved. You can avoid that by letting go of the past, forgiving people who hurt you, and if the Holy Spirit leads you, make an attempt at reconciliation. Sometimes you will resolve it with the other individual, and sometimes you must resolve it within yourself.

Take some time today to pray and ask God to reveal to you anyone who you should make things right with before it's too late. It's a very humbling experience, and it won't be easy, but believe me…you don't want the alternative. May your heart be made light.

READ TODAY: JAMES 4:14-17

DAY 93
IT'S A BIG FAMILY.
THEY GONE TAKE UP THE CENTER AISLE.

One thing black folks will do is try to predict what's going to happen at the funeral before it happens. We like to make guesses on who is going to do the eulogy and even on what venue will be used. "Well you know her home church was Mt. Zion, but they're probably gonna have it at the Faith Dome to fit all those people." That's usually when the size of the family starts getting estimated. "You know it's a big family. They gone need that whole center aisle just for the family.

That reminds me of a time in the Bible where God promised a big family to Abraham. He didn't have any children yet, but God told him that his descendants would be as numerous as the stars in the sky. He was promised a big family, but Abraham and his wife Sarah were getting up in age and still didn't even have one child. Many years went by, and they did some foolish things while waiting, but eventually God's promise did come true for them. They ended up with the biggest family ever. Like…you might be related to them. The story reminds us to wait for the promise. Don't be in such a hurry to try to make it happen on your own. God's timing isn't the same as ours. Allow your faith to make you **calm** and **patient** as you wait on God. If He said it, believe that He will do it!

READ TODAY: GENESIS 17:1-6

DAY 94
CELEBRATION OF LIFE/HOMEGOING/FUNE

We can't just be regular and call it a funeral. Nope. We have to give it a little razzle-dazzle. I remember watching the funeral for Coretta Scott King on TV. All the major news outlets were covering it, and I believe every living president at the time was present at the service. I remember one of the news anchors explaining to the general public what a "Celebration of Life" was. It was my first time realizing that this was a black thang!

No matter what you like to call it, I think we all need to understand that these bodies are only temporary. We are spirits, and our body of flesh can only contain us for so long. Jesus, however, promises that when we believe in Him, we will never truly die. Even in physical death, we have the assurance of everlasting life in the presence of God, our Father. Our time on earth isn't always easy. It's peppered with trials, tribulations, tears, sickness, pain, and sorrow. We all go through something down here. But we can be confident that when this body can no longer withstand, we can move to another building that wasn't made with hands. We will be changed, healed, and whole in the presence of the King. Let's be grateful today that even death cannot separate us from Him.

READ TODAY: 2 CORINTHIANS 5:1

DAY 95
I JUST TALKED TO HIM A COUPLE WEEKS AGO.

When we get the news that someone has passed away, one of the first things we do is try to remember our most recent conversation. We'll say things like… "Lawd hammercy! I just talked to him a couple weeks ago. He said he was trying to buy a boat, and we said we were gonna get together soon and go fishing!" Now that we are in the social media age, people have resorted to posting up screenshots of the last text conversation or of the phone log showing that they just spoke to the deceased for 20 minutes last Tuesday.

What happens when the person you used to talk to is no longer there? Actually, this devotion isn't just about death. It's really about new life. Because what happens when someone keeps trying to recall old conversations and bring up old things that you used to say and do before you gave your life to the Lord and became a new creature? That person is confused because they feel like it wasn't long ago that they were having a conversation with who you used to be. Some people are going to try hard to tempt you so that they can prove you are still the same person…that you're no better than you used to be back when. Resist the urge to fall into that trap. If they can't accept that you are no longer bound by Satan, you may have to love them from a distance. Let that marinate today.

READ TODAY: EPHESIANS 4:22

DAY 96
HE STAYED TO HIMSELF. HE AIN'T BOTHER NOBODY.

If you've ever heard this statement, it was probably made in reference to someone whose life was lost in a tragic and unfair way. Often, it is used when an innocent bystander dies at the hands of someone else's evil deeds and carelessness. Every now and again though, I'll see posts offering condolences and claiming that the deceased stayed to himself and didn't bother anybody. But when I click on his page, the profile tells a different story. I see him posted up with guns and money, holding up gang signs, and always wearing the same color.

I said all that to say, we really need to pray for our young black kids. As parents, family members, and people in the community, we can't be so self-absorbed that we miss these obvious signs that something is wrong. Some of these kids need help from us and some need help from a professional as well. We can't ignore it because it's hard work or because we don't want to ruffle anyone's feathers. We can't ignore it because "NoBOdY HeLPeD mE, aNd I TuRneD oUt fiNe..." Please everyone, if you know a young boy, girl, man, or woman, who has gone astray, make it your mission to pray for them and maybe even fast for their deliverance. The world would be a much better place if there was more prayer and less delusion.

READ TODAY: GALATIANS 6:2

DAY 97
IT'S PEOPLE DYING TODAY
THAT AIN'T NEVER DIED BEFORE.

I don't know who the first person was to say this phrase, but I commend them for this little golden nugget of a sentence. It's funny, but it's true. I've heard it in church a few times and even in movies.

When people die, it's always a new experience, not just for the family, but also for the deceased. We really don't have a lot of reliable information on what it feels like to die or be dead. All we know is that being absent from our body means being present with the Lord. That's honestly why I don't hang out in graveyards. No disrespect to those who do, but you know…your loved one isn't there. They are absent, quite literally. I had someone who argued me downnnnn that it's disrespectful to the deceased not to visit their grave. My rebuttal was that it's disrespectful to the deceased not to walk in your destiny and complete your God-given assignments while you have the time.

Anybody who cared about you isn't up in heaven mad because you didn't come sit for an hour with their physical remains on their birthday. Loose yourself from tradition and live a life that is fulfilled and ready to go be with the Lord whenever it's your turn. I know that's what my dad would want. He is present with the Lord and couldn't care any less about me standing around and talking to his grave, rehearsing the old things while missing out on the new thing that God wants to do in my life. Just food for thought.

READ TODAY: 2 CORINTHIANS 5:8-9

DAY 98
REPAST

After the funeral is complete and the body has been deposited at the gravesite, black funerals often end with a repast. Repast is just a fancy word that means "meal". Most repasts are held back at the church in the fellowship hall where the family and close friends can gather to eat and greet each other. Fried chicken, cake, and punch are usually involved, and **sometimes** the food tastes absolutely amazing.

Before Jesus was taken and crucified, he had a small repast with his disciples in an upper room. Not only did they eat and fellowship, but Jesus also decided to perform a very humbling act of service for his guys. He washed their feet. Some of the disciples were originally against it, but Jesus explained that if they didn't want Him to serve them, then He would no longer be affiliated with them. How powerful is that?

Today's message is for the people who don't know how to receive love. Always giving but never receiving anything is actually very toxic in a friendship or relationship of any sort. It's certainly not God's way, nor is it the example that Jesus set for us. If the ground of your heart is so hardened that it cannot receive the deposit of a seed, you are literally depriving someone of a harvest and of the joy that comes from being a giver. It's definitely more blessed to give than to receive, but don't ruin someone else's opportunity to be blessed as a giver simply because you never learned to receive.

READ TODAY: JOHN 13:8

DAY 99
LOOKS JUST LIKE HIMSELF...

When black people go to a funeral or to a funeral home to do a viewing, one of the highest compliments they can give to the funeral home is to say that the deceased looks just like themselves. Some will even go on to say, "Looked just like he was sleeping." This means that the funeral home did a great job on the makeup and presentation.

Do you look just like yourself? Are you walking confidently in your own God-given identity? Or are you a reflection of something or someone else? I remember meeting several young preachers in college. Some of these guys had their own thing going, but most of them seemed like they were trying to be someone else they had seen and admired. It's understandable to want to emulate greatness, but what happens when you don't leave room to still look like yourself?

Remember that time in the early 2000s when every other up-and-coming gospel singer was trying to sound like Kim Burrell? Whew. That was a rough time for our nation. Listen, I just want to encourage you and let you know that God made you to look just like yourself. It's not rocket science today. Your assignment was given to **you** for a reason. It's okay to do the work to improve yourself, but that doesn't mean morphing into an inauthentic copy of someone else. Just ask God to show you how to best use **yourself** for His glory.

READ TODAY: GALATIANS 6:4

DAY 100
LOOKED LIKE SHE WAS JUST SLEEP

As we mentioned yesterday, when black folks go to a funeral or viewing, they are always going to comment on how closely that person resembles their normal, healthy state. It's like we can't help it. When we say that someone looks like they are asleep, it is another great compliment to those who prepared the body.

There was a time in the Bible where a synagogue leader named Jairus came to Jesus to ask for healing for his sick daughter. Before they could return to the house, they received word that she had already passed away. Jesus told Jairus not to be afraid but to believe. They went down to the house and found a crowd of dramatic people crying and falling out. Jesus told them to chill out because the girl wasn't dead, but sleeping. They laughed at Jesus, and then He put them all out except the parents and the disciples He had with Him. He spoke to the girl and told her to get up. She got up and started walking around, and folks were shooketh.

The moral of today's story is that perhaps there is something great inside of you that you thought was dead, but it's only sleeping. I've written two devotionals prior to this one. Life began to life pretty hard on me, and I honestly thought that I couldn't write any more. So much stress and craziness was going on around me, that I figured my ability to write and create was dead and gone. Turns out, the gift wasn't dead but sleeping. Like Jesus did, we must dismiss the distractions, the drama, and the hinderances from our presence. Surround yourself with those who will believe with you, and then watch that thing rise up and get to moving again! Cheers to waking up! My God Today!

READ TODAY: MARK 5:35-42

DAY 101
CASKET SHARP

I always found it to be a bit morbid, but if a black person says that you are "casket sharp," that is actually a great compliment! You see, black folks like to bury their loved ones in either the very best clothes they owned, or in a new outfit all together. So if someone is "casket sharp," then they are looking pretty good! If you haven't heard this, maybe you've heard people say, "You look good enough to be buried!"

I understand the concept, but it also makes me a little sad. Why is it that our best look is reserved for the grave? At that point, it's too late to even matter what we put on our bodies. I thought Jesus came that we might have **life** more abundantly, not that we might look good in a casket. All of this makes me think about the fact that many of us forget all about our todays. We're always looking forward to blessings for the future and reserving our best for some later date and time when tomorrow isn't even promised to us. I have been guilty of being so focused on an abundant life in the future, that I forget to live an abundant life today. There is nothing wrong with planning. It is wise to do so. But let's all be more intentional and more aware concerning the daily abundance that we often ignore. Look around!

READ TODAY: JOHN 10:10

DAY 102
WELL, HAD HE BEEN SICK?

When we hear the news of someone's passing, one of our first questions is whether or not the person had been sick. I think that maybe we do this to determine just how hard the loss may be hitting the loved ones. When my dad passed, he had been sick and hospitalized for quite a while, so it gave me a little time to get my brain acclimated to the idea of his transition. But when someone passes very suddenly, the impact can be even more traumatic.

Have you had any sudden, unfortunate, and unexpected events to take place in your life? If you have, you may be experiencing trauma. The word "trauma" describes the emotional consequences caused by the impact of a distressing event. If you have ever taken a physics class, you already know that when you increase the *speed* of a collision, you increase its *impact*.

If you are dealing with something in life that hit you fast and hard, you have to be very intentional about asking God to help you manage the impact. Perhaps it was the loss of a loved one, a job, or a relationship. I've seen people whose lives have been completely thrown off because they could never emotionally move forward from one moment. And I get it! It's not easy. That's why you have to turn to a mighty God for strength, comfort, and guidance. It may have caught you off guard, but we have a God who never sleeps and is never surprised nor traumatized by any sequence of events that may occur. He will give you what you need so that you don't have to let life's sudden moments consume you forever.

READ TODAY: PSALM 91:1-5

DAY 103
GET ME A PROGRAM.

If you've ever been to a black funeral, you already know that the programs are hot commodities. First the family marches into the church, and when they are all seated, the programs get distributed to them first. After that, the rest of the "lowly" attendees are given programs until they run out. Sometimes the programs are so nice! They are these beautiful booklets filled with never-before-seen photos of the deceased along with his or her family. Some of these programs are truly touching tributes and keepsakes. That being said, you have to hope they printed out enough to go around. I've seen some people come close to blows over one. Those who find themselves unable to make it to the service will often ask a friend to get them a program, which is not always an easy task.

You're probably wondering where I'm going with this. Well I just want you to know that before you were born, God created a beautiful program for your life. He already knew the ups and downs you'd face. He knew about the loss, the grief, and the pain you'd experience. But He also knew about the love, joy, peace, and prosperity. He knew what you would accomplish, and He knew when you would make mistakes. Nothing about your program catches God by surprise.

Perhaps you are anxious about certain turns that your life seems to be taking. Why not turn to God for the answers you seek? He is the author of your story, and He has written it so beautifully. Trust God's process and His program.

READ TODAY: ISAIAH 46:10

DAY 104
THE FAMILY CAR

By now, I'm sure you're wondering why I'm going on and on about funerals in this segment. Well they are a big part of the black experience, and if talking about them triggers you, I sincerely apologize. Consider that Jesus has taken the sting away from death and has taken any victory away from the grave! So, as with anything else, we can take even a funeral and extract a message from it. Now... let me talk about the family car. This is a limousine (or multiple limousines) provided by the funeral home and designated for the immediate family of the deceased to be transported to the funeral, gravesite, repast, and then back home. There are often limited seats in the family car compared to the size of the actual family, and sometimes there are arguments concerning who gets to ride in them. But family cars are quite convenient because they can help a grieving family who shouldn't have to be focused on driving in their hour of bereavement.

The family cars ensure that the family is all together, in the same place, and headed in the same direction. The family arrives to the destination together and they depart together as one. I have some questions for you. Are you intentional about trying to unify your family? Are you intentional about sowing seeds of faith into your children and other family members? Are you intentional about making sure everyone arrives safely to their God-given destination? Do you teach them the truth of God, or do you practice a hands-off approach, leaving your family vulnerable to Satan's tricks and traps? When is the last time you sat down with your family, opened a Bible, talked, and prayed? My prayer is that you will be able to unify your family and sow the good seeds of love, support, and God's holy word. Do the very best you can to plant. But don't get frustrated if you don't see fruit yet. Only God can make the seeds grow.

READ TODAY: JOSHUA 24:15

DAY 105
REFLECTIONS

Some funerals have a portion of the program where pre-designated people share their fond memories (aka reflections) of the deceased. Other funerals just treat it like an open-mic night and allow anyone who wants to speak to get up there and ramble on. It's supposed to be limited to 2 minutes, but that rarely happens. These are the funerals that end up lasting for four hours.

The Bible mentions something about "reflections" in 1 Corinthians 13. It says that we look in a glass, but our view is dim. Perhaps the mirror is dirty, keeping us from seeing the reflections clearly. As an optometrist, I am inclined to tell you that sometimes we just don't see things clearly. I've seen a visual acuity chart humble people real quick! People come in thinking that their vision is great, only to realize they can barely see the letters. These are usually the husbands whose worried wives made an appointment for them.

Why am I saying this? I need you to humble yourself enough to know that you don't know it all and that your perspective can potentially be tainted and unclear without you realizing it. In order to see the true nature of a thing, we must rely on the Holy Spirit to be our Windex™. His guidance can clear away anything that blocks our clarity. When you pray, ask God to help you follow the Holy Spirit's guidance so that you can make clear judgements for your own life.

READ TODAY: 1 CORINTHIANS 13:12

DAY 106
RESOLUTIONS

When you attend a black funeral, there is often a segment of the program called "Resolutions." The resolutions are letters that usually come from a church, an organization, or a governmental body that are read aloud by a designee. These letters usually list several facts about the deceased. It may begin by making statements such as, "Whereas Brenda Marie Jenkins was a faithful member of Usher Board #3 for 30 years...". The resolution usually ends with a statement of action such as, "Be it resolved that Usher Board #3 will be renamed and henceforth be known as the Brenda M. Jenkins Gum-Snatching Authority."

When we hear about resolutions, we often think about the New Year's resolutions that people often don't keep. But what spiritual resolutions have you made for yourself? Where is your resolve? Faith without any action is dead, right? If I am believing by faith to be delivered from alcoholism, I have to resolve not to hang out at the bar after work every day, right?

Today, I want you to think of the areas in your life where you need to be more resolute. Ask God to grant you wisdom and help you to learn better discipline in those areas so you may avoid temptation.

READ TODAY: MATTHEW 26:41

DAY 107
"SPECIAL FRIEND"

If you read an obituary and see the term "special friend" being used, it requires you to put two and two together. If Lillie Mae passed away, you will read that she "leaves to cherish her memory" followed by the names of all her children, siblings, and grandchildren. Next, it will say that she leaves a "host of nieces and nephews." And lastly, tucked all the way at the end, it will say, "and one special friend, Mr. Willie Earl Palmer."

If you can't read between the lines, let me help you…Mr. Willie Earl was her man! Certain people knew, but for the most part, Lillie and Willie kept their relationship on the low. They knew about something that many people ignore today. It's a little something called discretion.

Discretion means using wisdom to determine when it's time to tell your business and when it isn't. There are a few times in the Bible where people's lack of discretion caused them some hardships. Think about Joseph who shared a dream with his brothers. They did everything they could to sabotage him and his future. Thankfully, God always has the final say. God used every adverse event to turn around and bless Joseph, but I often wonder if Joseph would have saved himself some trouble with a bit of discernment and discretion. We'll never know.

Do yourself a favor, and ask the Holy Spirit for guidance on who you can and cannot confide in. We don't operate from a place of fear, but we must operate from a place of wisdom, discernment, and discretion.

READ TODAY: PROVERBS 2:11

DAY 108
DOVE RELEASE

I don't know when dove releases gained popularity, but the funeral home basically learned this little trick where they can release a dove, and it will fly away momentarily before returning. They usually recite a beautiful poem just before letting go of the dove and hoisting it up in the air to fly away. Recently, there was a viral video where the person doing the release apparently gripped the dove too tightly while reciting the poem. He hoisted the bird up to the sky, but it came right back down and hit the ground, stiff as a board. It would appear that the poor thing had suffocated while waiting to be released.

In the Bible, the dove was invoked symbolically to describe how the Holy Spirit descended at the Baptism of Jesus. So just for illustrative purposes, let's say that the dove symbolizes the Holy Spirit. Is it possible that, just like the funeral director in the viral video, we suffocate the Holy Spirit's ability to "fly" freely in our lives? Are we so busy trying to be seen and heard ourselves that we ignore something so precious? Is it also possible that people confuse the purpose of the Holy Spirit and think it's just for a show? Are we shouting, dancing, running, and falling out all over the church and calling that the Holy Spirit? And I'm good for a shout/dance/run combo, but there's more to it than that.

The Holy Spirit has many more functions than some of us know. How are you falling out and speaking in tongues, but don't know how to be kind to your spouse? Why can't you discern good from evil in that situation? When things happen in life, why are you so inconsolable when the Holy Spirit is a comforter? I'll have you read the fruit of the Spirit as food for thought. I pray that you will rethink the role that the Holy Spirit should play in the life of a believer.

READ TODAY: GALATIANS 5:22-23

DAY 109
CLOSE THE CASKET

As we end the series on black folks at funerals, I have to mention this part of the service. The closing of the casket gives you an idea on what direction everything else is about to go. Once the family has marched in, viewed their loved one in the casket, and taken their seats, it is now time to close the casket and proceed with the service. If the casket closes, and everyone remains calm, you can probably get out of there in 90 minutes or less. If, however, the funeral directors start closing the casket, and one (all it takes is one) family member goes to hootin', hollering, crying, and falling over the casket...it catches on like wildfire. The rest of the family that was trying to hold it in will now begin to lose it too. At this point, there is a strong possibility that the choir members up in the choir stand will start their waterworks as well. THAT funeral will be 3 hours minimum.

Well, I just stopped by to tell somebody today that it's time to close the casket on those things that have been negatively impacting your life. Are there things that you have allowed to linger on even though they died a long time ago? Do you keep looking back to the past and wondering when things will return to the way they were? Newsflash! Things are never going to be what they were. They are going to be so much better! But first, you have to let go of the funeral director's arm, back away from the casket, and accept that the past has served its purpose. Do not stand there mourning it so much that you miss the next move of God in your life! Trust God enough to gracefully close that chapter and begin your next one today!

READ TODAY: ISAIAH 43:18-19

DAY 110
TOO BLESSED TO BE STRESSED

Whew! Okay. I'm done with the black funeral-speak. I had more, but I didn't want to run you all away. But for today, let's look at this phrase that most of us have heard an auntie say. The phrase "too blessed to be stressed," gained a lot of popularity in the 80s and 90s. It was catchy, it rhymed, and it was true. It only makes sense that it had our people in a chokehold.

I **know** I'm too blessed to be stressed, yet I still find myself feeling stressed out far too often. Stress wreaks havoc on our health. I find that when I am stressed out, either I have an improper perspective on something, or I have not placed the proper boundaries around it. There are plenty of things to be grateful for, but when I am stressed, I'm too focused on the things that are not going my way instead of praising God for the wonderful blessings that I take for granted. Focusing on gratitude and finding more things to thank God for can serve as a powerful stress reliever.

If you're experiencing high levels of stress, I recommend that you pray and ask the Holy Spirit for guidance on setting proper boundaries in your life. We must learn to say "no" to things that God never instructed us to **do, be, or have.** Not setting godly boundaries can be very stressful, even when you have the best intentions. That's why the Bible tells us to pray about everything. So if you find yourself consistently stressed out about life, you have some changes to make, because that is not God's will for your life. You're too blessed.

READ TODAY: PROVERBS 10:22

DAY 111
FIRST, GIVING HONOR TO GOD...

If you are ever called upon to get on the mic during a black, Baptist church service, this is the unofficial/official way to start it off. It's not a real rule, but we all know what it is. Once you have gotten this out of the way, you can deliver the remainder of your content. You will hear this a lot when someone gets up to tell a testimony.

Although it became a cliché church phrase, you can't be mad at the sentiment behind it. They were basically saying, "Before I do anything, let me acknowledge, reverence, and respect God." I can get jiggy with that, because that's honestly how we should be living our lives all around. God should be the first priority not just in our words, but in our deeds also.

Life taught me that people make time for what they care about, and they make excuses for what they don't. Do you read the gossip blogs but say that the Bible is too confusing even with a million translations? Do you get halfway through your day without even speaking to God first? Listen, there will always be a distraction. There will always be something that seems more pressing than your spiritual well-being. Don't fall for it! Honor God FIRST and watch the rest fall in line.

READ TODAY: PROVERBS 3:9-10

DAY 112
...WHO IS THE HEAD OF MY LIFE.

This is the follow up to yesterday's devotion. After "First giving honor to God...," we go on to clarify who He is to us. The full phrase is, "First giving honor to God, who is the head of my life." I don't know who was the first to use this phrase, but it caught on like wildfire.

The only thing better than this cliché church phrase, is when it's actually true. When something or someone is "the head," it means that they are in charge. Think about the body. All of the main decision-making entities of the body are found in the head. If you need to determine which way to go, that decision isn't made by your feet. It's made by the eyes, ears, nose, and brain, which are all found in your head.

So if God is the head of your life, it means that what you do or don't do, should be determined by Him. If you let your feet decide where to walk without first listening to your eyes, ears, nose, and brain, you could walk directly into a housefire. Imagine trying to drive your car while hanging upside down. Your head is on the floor and your feet are on the steering wheel. You can't possibly see, hear, or think to drive safely that way, and you look foolish! Could you be doing that with your life? My prayer is that we will stop the power struggle with God, and let the Head be the head.

READ TODAY: LUKE 6:46

DAY 113
BUILDING FUND

If you grew up in a black church, you may have heard of the building fund. There was always a spot on the offering envelope to give money to this building fund. As a kid, I remember thinking there would eventually be a new building, paid for with these funds. I began to wonder when and if the building would ever be built. It wasn't until later that I realized our "building fund" was really used to pay for the mortgage, maintenance, and repairs on the "building" we already had. (I had been confusing *building*, the verb with *building* the noun.)

There was a time in the Old Testament where they had issues with the building fund. That's right. Haggai, the prophet, was sent to let God's people know that they were messing up. The temple of God was literally in ruins, and they were supposed to be building it back up. Instead, they took their money and balled out with it while the temple of God was still over there looking a hot mess. They were building nice homes for themselves but procrastinating when it came to doing something to honor the Lord.

The word from Haggai was "consider your ways." He told them that no matter how much money they made, it would never be enough, because God, Himself would see to it that other issues would continue to come up and drain their pockets. This would be the case until they prioritized Him. The moral of the story is that if you work hard but can never seem to get ahead, consider your ways. Are you truly putting God's assignments first?

READ TODAY: HAGGAI 1:1-10

DAY 114
HE WOKE ME UP THIS MORNING
AND STARTED ME ON MY WAY.

You may have heard this phrase either spoken by someone at church or as a lyric to a gospel song. It has been heavily used by singers and preachers in black churches for decades now.

I don't know about you, but I'm feeling pretty grateful today. One thing about the older saints is that they had less but were more grateful. It seems like the more we advance as a people, the more money we get, and the more houses we build, the less grateful we are. How backwards is that? Our ancestors were grateful for something as simple as being allowed to wake up every morning, and here we are complaining because the Mercedes maintenance is so expensive. Well…not we…y'all…because I don't have a Mercedes (…yet. But I still believe God. Ha!).

All I want you to do today is find some things that **seem** small but are actually big. Perhaps you have taken for granted the fact that you can take a deep breath. There are so many who wish they could. Perhaps you have taken for granted the fact that you have plumbing and running water. Let's challenge ourselves to go through today without complaints. Every time you find yourself wanting to complain, think about one of those small-big things and give God praise.

READ TODAY: LAMENTATIONS 3:22-23

DAY 115
HE PUT FOOD ON MY TABLE.

After the old saints finished thanking God for waking us up and starting us on our way, the very next thing would be to thank Him for putting food on our table. I love this gratitude for the simple things, yet they are only simple to us because we are so blessed! There are some people who only wish they had food to eat, much less a table to actually eat it on.

There was a time in the Bible where the children of Israel had to wander around in the desert for 40 years because of their initial refusal to obey God and enter their promised land. I'm sure it was a crazy time, but God literally provided all of their basic needs while they were out there. He provided them with food from heaven. No...I mean literally. Every morning when they woke up, there was new/fresh food on the ground called manna. They could collect it and eat it raw or prepare it as cakes/bread. It was only good for that one day before it went bad and the supply had to be replenished. They had no other choice than to trust God for their daily bread. My God Today!

The children of Israel had to be totally dependent upon God, and we must learn to do the same. Have you placed more confidence in your education, job, career, or ability to work hard than you have placed in God? It only takes an instant for your world to change. I don't speak anything unfortunate happening to anyone, but when you start putting faith, trust, and hope in other things, you are making an idol god, which is dangerous. God won't have it. He may have to remove it in order to show you the **true** source of your daily bread. Today, let's pray and ask God to show us anything we may be placing ahead of Him.

READ TODAY: DEUTERONOMY 8:3

DAY 116
HE PUT CLOTHES ON MY BACK
AND SHOES ON MY FEET.

I could go on for days about the things that the old saints would be sure to thank God for. We're living in a time where people barely want to wear the same outfit more than once, and yet we struggle to be grateful. Meanwhile, the old saints were thanking God for backs that were simply covered and not naked.

I'm going to talk about the children of Israel again today. When they were walking around the wilderness for 40 years getting their daily bread, do you know what else they got? They had clothes and shoes that never wore out. That's a miracle indeed! I imagine that as they grew, the clothes grew with them. Yesterday, we talked about the bread and God's provision, but one thing we don't talk about enough is God's **preservation.** Have you ever been in a situation where something could have and should have depleted you, but it didn't? That's preservation. Have you ever been in a situation where you should have lost your mind, but you didn't? That's preservation. Have you ever been in a situation where you should have looked like a reflection of the struggles you've been through, but you didn't? That, my friend, is preservation.

I think we ought to spend some time today thanking God for how He has preserved us down through the years!

READ TODAY: PSALMS 40:11

DAY 117
HIGHWAYS AND BYWAYS

When the old saints would pray, they'd always thank God for keeping them safe on the highways and byways. I guess I'm too young to know what a byway is, so I had to look it up. A byway is a road or track that doesn't follow a main route. Byways are "off the beaten path," and may even lack paving.

I too, am grateful that God has kept me safe on the highways and byways. And I'm not just referring to the actual roadways. Sometimes you find yourself on a highway in life. You're on a main road, clearly headed in the right direction towards your destination. But there are other times when you may get off-track and find yourself on one of life's byways instead. Have you ever ended up on a rocky road that you never imagined yourself traveling? Maybe it was a bad relationship, a divorce, an addiction, a large debt, or maybe even some legal trouble. Thank God that He was still there with you. His grace and mercy followed you and helped you get back on the right road.

Aren't you glad that God is more powerful that one wrong turn? Aren't you glad that He knows how to reroute and restore us to our intended destination? God is good. Let's thank God today that even when we strayed away from the planned path, He didn't leave us to navigate it alone.

READ TODAY: PSALM 16:11

DAY 118
IF I CAN'T SAY A WORD, I'LL JUST WAVE MY HAND.

You can step into most any black church today, and if someone gets on the mic and says "If I can't say a word…" the congregation will respond by simply waving their hands. It's like the church equivalent of "…just wave your hands in the air! Wave 'em like you just don't care!"

I recently suffered from the loss of my grandfather. Rev. Dr. J.W. Croom, Jr. was the best, most consistent man I've ever known. He was the man who baptized me, and he was my first pastor. I can honestly say that he was the same person at home that he was at church. I have so much admiration for grandaddy. My dad (his son) passed about 10 years ago, so grandaddy was the man I had present in my life for the longest amount of time. He was very big on studying God's word and is responsible for the majority of the Christian education that I received from a young age. If you benefit from this book, you have benefited from my grandfather's seeds. Pray for me y'all. It's hard, but I'm comforted in knowing that he lived such a full life. He had good health and lived at his house on his own until the last 6 months of his life. And out of his 94.8 years, he was only truly "down" for the last 6 days of it.

In those last days, he suffered from pneumonia and couldn't really communicate verbally. We gathered around his hospital bed one night and sang some of his favorite hymns. The Spirit of the Lord was present with us, and as I was holding his hand, he lifted it high in the air. Everyone thought I was raising his hand for him, when actually, he was raising mine. He couldn't say a word, so he waved his hand. I understand it now. God is worthy to be praised at all times, in all ways, and in all circumstances. Even when it's hard to do, **find a way to do it.**

READ TODAY: PSALMS 63:4-7

DAY 119
VIADOC/VI-DOC/VIADUCT

Since we're talking about my grandfather (see yesterday), let me introduce you to one of his favorite words. Depending on your age and where you're from, you may be familiar with a "viadoc." The correct spelling is "viaduct," but that doesn't matter. A viadoc is an elevated bridge-like structure, usually consisting of several supporting arches, used to carry a road or railroad across a valley or other lower ground level. And although it's not the exact same thing, many older black people will refer to a highway overpass as a "viadoc." Whenever they give driving directions (because they don't care about your GPS), they will always reference said viadoc. "You're going to go down about 2 more miles...now if you get to the **viadoc,** you went too far." "You're going to go up under the **viadoc** and make a left at that stop sign..."

The purpose of the viadoc structure is to allow you to pass over a low place. My God Today! I had a lot more to say, but it just hit me that Jesus is our viadoc! When we were lost in sin, Jesus came and took the penalty. He became our way over, our overpass. Remember when the Israelites were in slavery in Egypt, and it was the lamb's blood on the doorpost that allowed the plague of death to "pass over" their homes? Well listen, that was symbolic for what Jesus would eventually come and do for us. He became the "Lamb" of God, and when His blood was shed on Calvary, it allowed the deathly consequences of our sin to pass over us on a viadoc named Jesus. He **is** the bridge that kept us from having to go to a low place. Whew! Are you covered today? Is your house covered? They don't want you to talk about Jesus anymore. His name alone is so powerful, it makes demons tremble. But let's all thank Jesus today for being our viadoc over sin, guilt, shame, and condemnation!

READ TODAY: JOHN 1:29

DAY 120
I'M JUST GLAD TO BE SEEN AND NOT VIEWED.

As I've said before, black folks love to add the razzle dazzle to almost everything. One such thing is how we respond when someone asks how we are doing. Sure, responses like, "I'm fine, thank you…" would easily suffice. But why say that when you could say something as awesome as, "I'm just glad to be seen and not viewed."? If you haven't heard this saying before, you may not fully understand its meaning. We are basically saying that we are glad to be alive. We are grateful that you didn't have to come view our body in a casket at a funeral service.

We talked a lot recently about how black people act when it comes to death and funerals. But can we just pause for a moment today to be grateful for life and a reasonable portion of health and strength? Because if you still have breath in your body, it's not too late for you to make a change. What is that thing that you know you're supposed to be doing that you keep putting off? Is it a health thing? Maybe it's a career thing, or even a ministry thing. Are you supposed to be going back to school? Are you supposed to be changing your diet and going back to the gym? Are you supposed to be forgiving someone? Going to therapy? Whatever it is, tomorrow isn't promised, and none of us know how many days we have left. Your best course of action is to obey God **today.** I'll start by finishing this book that God gave me to write. Life has been throwing so much at me lately, and sometimes the struggle makes it hard to create. But if God told me to do it, I have to stop making excuses and acting as if I have unlimited time. So if you have this book in your hand, praise God that I finally got it together and obeyed. I challenge you to do the same!

READ TODAY: PSALMS 90:12

DAY 121
MY BAD.

When someone says, "my bad," it is an apology. The phrase is more commonly used amongst young black men. If, for instance, a guy was to accidentally step on someone's foot, he might turn around and say, "Oh, my bad." Back in the 1990s, stepping on someone's fresh new kicks was quite literally enough to get you killed (I know it sounds crazy, but the 90s was a wild time). Sometimes, a quick and sincere "Oh, my bad…" was enough to save your life.

And it's the same to this day. There are countless relationships that are unnecessarily "killed" or ripped apart because people don't know how to humble themselves and simply apologize. I think a lot of us have trouble admitting out loud that we are imperfect. But we have to understand that even with the purest of intentions, we can all make a mistake. We can all fall short. It's important to apologize and admit "your bad" to anyone who may have been affected by your misstep. That person may or may not forgive, but that is on them. All you can do is your own part. God cares that you have done your part. Ask the Holy Spirit to reveal to you anyone who may need an apology from you. We can also ask for help on how to go about doing it. Let this be your reminder.

READ TODAY: MATTHEW 5:23-24

DAY 122
NAH, YOU GOOD.

"Nah, you good..." is the desired outcome of yesterday's devotion. When you apologize for something, you are hoping that the person will forgive you for whatever offense you have caused. Let's use the same example from yesterday about stepping on someone's fresh new kicks in the 90s. It was a very tense moment, because people were really crazy then. But once you have apologized, and that tough-looking individual looks at you and says, "Nah, you good..." it's a whole sigh of relief. Whew! You will live to see another day!

Well sometimes we will do things that are sinful or offensive towards God. But I'm so glad to report that you don't have to worry about Him holding some crazy grudge over you. When we confess to God what we've done, repent, and ask for forgiveness, He is so faithful that not only does He grant us the forgiveness, but He also turns us around and cleans us up so that the stain of our sin is no longer present or visible on our lives. Wow! That is such a blessing.

I really hate to see so many people painting God as perpetually angry and filled with wrath 24/7. God is love, and although He hates sin for us, He doesn't hate us for sin. Read that again. He's so faithful in His relationship to us that He forgives and cleanses us even though we were unfaithful to Him. When we repent (change our mindset about the behavior) and ask for forgiveness, He picks us up, dusts us off, and says, "Nah, you good." That's a good place to praise Him today!

READ TODAY: 1 JOHN 1:9

DAY 123
MANNISH

As a child, I would hear older people use this word. I thought it was made-up, but it's actually in the dictionary. Apparently, it means just what it says. Someone who is being mannish is acting like a man. Yup, I was overthinking it, but that's because in the black community, when a girl (but sometimes a boy) is called mannish, she is considered to have bad manners and/or to be sexually promiscuous. In other words, she is not lady-like. It's not a compliment.

The negative implications of the word reflect the lowered standards/expectations that some people set and accept for men. "Boys will be boys." Meanwhile, women are expected to be this beautiful, virtuous, loving, patient, kind, caring, faithful, hard-working individual who stands on business, gets her bag, holds everybody down, knows how to do everything, and looks fine doing it. She is to do and be all of this, while often being treated less-than in the world. That kind of pressure seems unfair!

I don't know how to change the way society views/treats women, but I can give a word of wisdom to the men and women reading this. Men, if you have a good, God-fearing woman in your life, use your words **and** actions to show her that she is loved, honored, and respected. And women, don't wait around for a pat on the back that may never come. God sees you, and He will reward you for your faithfulness in due time. Rely on His strength, because yours isn't enough.

READ TODAY: PROVERBS 31: 25-30

DAY 124
SEE WHAT HAD HAPPENED WAS...

If you ask a black person for an explanation on a particular matter, and they begin with this phrase, you already know it's about to be some foolishness. Everything said after that will be an excuse.

Parent: Jamarcus! Why do you have a "D" in Social Studies?

Jamarcus: See what had happened was…the teacher don't like me because I'm black. And when I tried to turn in my project, I dropped it, and it broke…oh, and I couldn't turn in my work because I couldn't remember my locker combination.

Jesus told a parable about this once. There was a wealthy man who was leaving town for a while. He had his servants to hold on to some of his money while he was gone. The monetary denomination they used in that day was called a "talent." To one servant, he gave five talents; to another three; and to another one. The servants with the five and the three talents took the money, invested it, and grew it for the man before he returned. The servant with one talent did absolutely nothing with his, and didn't have any increase. When asked why, he came up with all these lame excuses… "See what had happened was…". The master was livid and literally went off on Him.

So are you growing the value of what you've been given, or are you making excuses for staying the same? If you're still reading this book, my guess is that you're growing! Be a good steward and stick with it. This time next year, I am believing that you will be experiencing even higher heights and deeper depths in God.

READ TODAY: MATTHEW 25:19-30

DAY 125
LIKED'TA

"Liked'ta" is a (southern) black people synonym for "almost." If you liked'ta do something, it means that you were very close to doing it, but you didn't. Someone might say, for example, "I liked'ta fainted when I saw my crush in a 3-piece suit."

My dad used to tell me that "almost" only counts in horseshoes and hand grenades, which I thought was pretty funny. There was a time in the Bible where Paul had been arrested for preaching the gospel. He went before King Agrippa to tell his story and plead his case. Once he was done, the king was so moved by his words, that he basically told Paul, "Wow...you almost had me believing too!" But like my dad said, this ain't horseshoes nor is it hand grenades.

When you decide to follow Christ, it's imperative that you trust and believe in Him with your whole heart. It's hard to walk fully in the promises of God when you still have doubts that He is able to deliver on them. If you want to believe God for something, but you're struggling with doubt, I suggest that you look back at all the ways He has come through for you in the past. Faith is truly a journey. Our faith should get stronger each time He performs or keeps His word. The problem is that we often allow current trials and tribulations to make us forget the past victories. Take some time today to remember when God came through for you just when you liked'ta quit.

READ TODAY: HEBREWS 11:6

DAY 126
THAN A MUG/LIKE A MUG

"A mug" is a well-known African American unit of measurement. Although you won't find it in any textbooks, "than a mug" is widely understood to mean "very much" or "to a great degree." If someone says, for example, "I haven't eaten all day, I'm hungry than a mug..." we know that this person is absolutely famished. The measuring scale goes **slightly < kinda < than a mug**. To answer your question, no, there is not an actual mug or measuring cup involved. Rather, the phrase is a phonetic adaptation of a less appropriate phrase that we will not discuss here today.

The Bible speaks of measuring when it talks about judgement. In Matthew 7, we are warned about judging others without considering that we will also be judged in return. It goes on to say that whichever measuring stick we choose to judge others with, is the same measuring stick that we will have to stand next to as well. This passage is really talking about hypocrites. Sadly, we are living in a highly hypocritical society today. People get online judging, pointing fingers, shaming, and canceling people whose issues have been exposed, never considering that they, themselves, are one false move away from being in a similar situation.

Let's not be like that. We don't know exactly what's going on in another person's heart, and we don't know what series of events led them to the place where they are now. Everything is so cut, dry, black, and/or white when it comes to someone else's problems. But when it comes to us, we want everyone to consider the various shades of grey. Today, I remind you to do unto others as you would have them do unto you.

READ TODAY: MATTHEW 7:1-5

DAY 127
NO HOME TRAINING

Have you ever seen a kid who had no manners? Things were a bit different back in the 90s. Back then, we were expected to be respectful and mannerable, especially in public. If we wanted to cut loose, we were supposed to do it in the privacy of our own homes. Whenever black folks saw children misbehaving in public, they'd look, shake their heads, and say three words… "No home training."

When I left for college, I quickly realized how many of my peers had not been trained at home. I was a little more judgey back then. "No home training…" I'd say to myself whenever I'd see some of the recklessness. Since then, many more parents have decided on a more "uninvolved" parenting style. Some of them are afraid to ruffle feathers with their own kids. Others fear disciplining their kids, because they don't want to lose them as friends. Still other parents are too busy living their best lives to share any wisdom with their children. The Bible tells parents to train children in the right way, and when they grow up, they will stick with it. I just want to encourage parents and future parents today. Keep doing what's right with your kids. You may not see the fruit now, but those good seeds that you have sown, will eventually grow. Be intentional, and don't give up on them. Continue to pray and sow seeds on behalf of those kids. You won't regret it.

READ TODAY: PROVERBS 22:6

DAY 128
WHO MADE THE MAC & CHEESE?

Let's not beat around the bush here. When it comes to the Mac and to the Cheese, black folks do not play! Nobody cares about your feelings. Decorum goes out the window. We are not tiptoeing around it. We need to know who made the mac and cheese, so that we can set our expectations where they need to be. There's nothing worse than helping yourself to a hefty serving of something that looks good, only to find out it's actually nasty.

Knowing who made the dish is even more important than how the dish looks. And that's our devotion everybody! Y'all have a blessed day! Oh wait… perhaps I should explain a little more. We have to **stop** judging people and situations by what they look like on the surface and **start** asking who is responsible for it. Who is this situation made by? Perhaps it looks good, but did Satan prepare this dish to throw me off track? Excuse me sir/ma'am, I know you're fine and all, but where did you come from exactly? Were you prepared for me by God, or are you just a good-looking distraction? Who is responsible for what is inside of you beneath the surface? These are questions that always need to be at the forefront of every new opportunity. Pray and ask God for wisdom and discernment. Ask Him if this was something He made for you, or if it was something made in hell's kitchen.

READ TODAY: 1 SAMUEL 16:7

DAY 129
I'M TRYING TO WATCH MY STORIES!

If you've ever been kept by your grandmother, you probably know how she was about her "stories." They never did call them soap operas, just stories. Grandma didn't ask for much, but when it was time for those stories to come on, you had better get on out of her face. My grandmother had a routine for her stories. All of her cooking and housework revolved around *General Hospital*, *The Young & the Restless*, and *The Bold & The Beautiful*.

One thing about Jesus, He too, loved Himself a good lil' story. He called them parables. He would often tell simple stories to His disciples or to a crowd in order to illustrate a more complex truth. These stories made God's principles easier to understand. One of my favorite stories was the parable of the sower.

The parable of the sower is about someone who is sowing the same type of seed on different types of soil and receiving various results. The seeds represent the word of God, and the soil represents the various conditions of the hearts of people who hear the word. The whole story is simply genius! You MUST read it. As a matter of fact, we will cut this devotion short to give you time to read the passage and meditate on it. Even if you've read it before, check it out again today and see if you can determine which soil represents you.

READ TODAY: MATTHEW 13: 1-13

DAY 130
GINGER ALE, *THE PRICE IS RIGHT*, & *GENERAL HOSPITAL*

To an outsider looking in, these three things have absolutely nothing to do with each other. But I'm willing to bet that many of you know what this is. This is the "I stayed home sick from school at my grandma's house" starter pack. If you ever had this experience, those were some of the BEST days! Once grandma got you some chicken noodle soup, Premium Crackers, and ginger ale (or gin-jail, as we like to pronounce it) in your system, you were STRAIGHT. By about 10am, you were healed, whole, and free to spend the rest of the day vibing with granny and watching Bob Barker on the *Price Is Right* before settling in for her favorite stories (aka soap operas).

What is today's message even about? I don't know…how about rest? Half the time, that's all we really needed anyway. Even as children with loads of energy, sometimes we needed to unplug from our normal daily grind (that perfect attendance award was a scam). So what makes us think that we, as adults, should go without the rest that God literally ordained for us to take? When you are tired, your flesh knows that it can get away with more and blame it on the fatigue. "It's been a long week. I deserve a little _____." I'll let you fill in the blank, but it's usually something you don't need. A moment of undisciplined fatigue can result in a lifetime of consequences. God demonstrated rest for us in Genesis. A day of rest was also included in the Ten Commandments, and even Jesus would steal away to pray and rest. If all you do is grind, I urge you to pray and ask God for a better strategy for provision (or perhaps for wisdom on how to do more with what you already have). Remember, He is more than able to provide everything you need, including rest!

READ TODAY: EXODUS 33:14

DAY 131
YA MAMA

Has anyone ever cracked a joke on you so bad that you just couldn't come up with the comeback fast enough? When that happens, most people know they can resort to simply saying, "Ya Mama." This means that whatever cruel thing that person just said to you, will now be applied to their own mother. When an enemy invokes your mother, it is extremely personal and triggering. This often leads to violence, so don't try it at home.

Today, let's talk about one of the most famous mamas of all time. When I think about Mary, the mother of Jesus, I think about strength and courage. When the angel came to inform her of what was to come, she was afraid at first, but she stood on business and said, "Be it unto me according to Thy word." That statement is so powerful to me, and I pray to live a life that says, "Be it unto me according to Thy word!" In other words, "Lord…if that's what You say, I'm down." Think about it. Who does that remind you of? In the garden of Gethsemane, Jesus was facing the worst emotional struggle of His life, and what did He say? "Nevertheless, not my will, but Thine be done."

Whew! I don't know if y'all know how powerful this devotion already is. I want to run a lap, but I don't want to lose my train of thought. It's time to stop trying to force your way onto God. Just stop! Our will compared to His is ridiculous. I get it. You had your plans, and you wanted this and that right now, and you can't wait. But look…the most powerful things in history happened when a mama and then a son said, "Lord, if that's what you want…cool."

READ TODAY: LUKE 1:38

DAY 132
A LIE DON'T CARE WHO TELL IT.

I'm not exactly sure where this phrase comes from, but I reckon it to be the truth. I tell ya, this world is full of lies. Everywhere we turn, we don't know what's true and what's fabricated. There are whole "news" organizations committed to skewing the truth for money, ratings, and political alliances. There are government agencies putting out information to the public to produce a desired outcome or even as a distraction to something else going on. There is even artificial intelligence being used now where fake videos can be made using another person's face and voice. The videos look so real, but it was all done on a computer. It's a frightening thought to think you could receive a fraudulent message appearing to be from someone you trust.

Lies are demonic tools used by Satan in his strategy to defeat us, and sadly they are everywhere. Satan doesn't care who tells his lie, as long as he can get you to believe it. He'll use anyone who is vulnerable to him in that moment. That's why it's never smart to put 100% of your hope or trust in man. Even your sweet Granny Pearl could be repeating something to you that simply isn't true. A lie doesn't care who takes hold of it and tells it. That's why it's so important to ask God for wisdom and discernment concerning people. Ask God to reveal the truth to you plainly. Once He does, don't pretend like you're confused. Act accordingly.

READ TODAY: PSALMS 118:8

DAY 133
YOU AIN'T NEVER LIED.

Sometimes someone says a statement so utterly true, that a simple "That's true" just isn't good enough. To add some razzle dazzle, we exclaim, "You ain't never lied!" Now of course we have no clue if this person has ever lied before, but what the heck?! Let's just take it to the extreme.

A wise person once said, "People lie, numbers lie…God don't." Okay, it's me. I said it. Most people would say that numbers don't lie, but I disagree. Have you ever been low on money? According to the numbers, you didn't have enough. But according to God, you had everything you needed! Have you ever gotten some test scores back that said you failed? According to the numbers, you weren't supposed to make it. But according to God, you passed the class and went on to graduate. If any of that has ever happened to you, you know it was nothing but the grace of God that brought you through.

God is the only One who has not and will not ever lie. Why? Because He doesn't just speak the truth. He **is** the truth. Satan is the one who lies and tries to deceive you into thinking that what God says isn't true. He is the father of lies. He is the originator of lies. Don't fall for them. God, on the other hand, **ain't never lied**, and He's not about to start today with you! Have some faith.

READ TODAY: NUMBERS 23:19

DAY 134
THAT'S WHAT I NEED TO BE DOING.

Have you ever been somewhere minding your own business when you see another black person, either walking, jogging, or biking past you for exercise? I don't know where it comes from, but there's always this strong African American urge to say, "That's what I need to be doing." You might say it to yourself, or if you're feeling particularly friendly, you may actually say it out loud to that person.

When Jesus lived on earth, He set the best possible example for this human experience of ours. He showed us how to love, how to deal with haters, how to suffer, how to pray, how to stay connected to God, how to use the word in our daily lives, how to humble ourselves, and so much more. Whenever I read the gospels and see how Jesus lived, I think, "that's what I need to be doing." Please don't let people fool you. Jesus isn't what they make him out to be. Read Matthew, Mark, Luke, and John for yourself, and you will see the awesome example that He really set for us. Let's thank God today for how He not only told us what we need to be doing, but He also showed us when He sent Jesus. And let's praise Him one mo' time today for the gift of the Holy Spirit, who enables us to do those things that need to be done!

READ TODAY: 1 PETER 2:21

DAY 135
I'M JUST GOING TO SHOW MY FACE.

Have you ever been invited somewhere that you honestly did not feel like going? You knew, however, that your presence would mean a lot to the person who invited you. You wanted to show your support, so you made it up in your mind that you would go briefly enough to do just that. When black people do this, we say, "I'm just going to show my face."

When it comes to our relationship with God, one of the best things we can do is seek His face. The Bible mentions this on several occasions, but what does it mean for God to show us His very face? It's not His literal face that we are looking to see. Any good relationship is going to include two people who have taken the time to truly get to know one other. Well God already knows us completely, so that just leaves us being the ones who need to get to know Him better. When we are interested in seeing the face of God, it means we are interested in discovering His features. Who is He? What is His character? How does He like to operate? It's important to know these things, because when life hits, and you don't know His character, you're in for a time! You'll be overwhelmed with fear and worry. You'll make poor decisions out of fear. And some may even embrace unhealthy habits as coping mechanisms. You'll tear apart at the seams, and Lord, don't let me get on the little number that grief will do on you!

My prayer for you and for all of God's people is that we would stop spending all of our time trying to get Him to show us His hand (blessings, gifts, prosperity), but instead spend more time trying to find His face.

READ TODAY: PSALMS 27:8

137

DAY 136
GET SOMEWHERE AND SADDOWN.

If your parents or grandparents ever used this phrase with you, it meant that you were doing too much, and they were fed up. Once you have kids of your own, you can truly relate to what your folks were saying. All that running around, making a mess, being loud, opening and closing the refrigerator door, and messing with stuff you had no business messing with, is highly irritating. This phrase was particularly common during a storm or other weather-related issue that prevented the kids from going outside to release their energy for the day. We were told to get somewhere and saddown (sit down).

Sometimes as adults, we really need to get somewhere and sit down. Is it possible that you're doing too much? Could we be running around, making messes, and getting into stuff that we have no business getting into? Could we be too loud in situations where we would be better off choosing silence? Are we opening and/or closing doors that God never told us to touch? I understand that faith without works is dead, but that doesn't mean we are to be busybodies who never sit still enough to hear the voice of God and yield to His way of handling the situations at hand. Even Jesus had to get somewhere and sit down sometimes to pray, to stay connected to God, and to make sure His flesh wasn't rising up over His spirit. If Jesus had to do that, what makes us think that we don't? If we can't relax and put our cares in God's hands, then what does that say about our faith? I'm telling ya…you're going to wear yourself out not trusting God. Today, let's all try to get somewhere with Him and saddown.

READ TODAY: PSALMS 46:10-11

DAY 137
I BROUGHT YOU IN THIS WORLD,
I CAN TAKE YOU OUT!

This is a very well-known black mama threat. Thankfully, my mother never used it on me, but I have definitely heard it used in pop culture and elsewhere. It's used to let a child know that their parents are not to be trifiled with. If you hear this phrase, it is your warning to get it together lest there be strong consequences and repercussions for your actions.

Unless they are crazy, this is an exaggeration. They aren't planning to actually take away the very life that they ushered you into. But this reminds me of a man named Job in the Bible. He was a great man, and yet God allowed him to go through some extremely difficult tragedies at the hand of Satan. All of his friends told him that God was punishing him for something, and that maybe he would do better to turn his back on God and give up on life all together. He told his friends that sometimes the Lord gives to us and sometimes He takes away from us, but either way… "blessed be the name of the Lord." Job didn't turn his back on God, and he didn't give up on life. Eventually, God would restore Job and bless him with even more than he already had, so be encouraged today! God has a plan for everything, even for your suffering. He's still in control, and He can restore everything plus more! Just hold on to your faith. Don't let go of God's unchanging hand!

READ TODAY: JOB 1:21

DAY 138
YOU'RE IN CHARGE TILL I GET BACK.

There comes a time in a kid's life where their parents feel comfortable enough with their maturity level to leave them at home alone without direct supervision. If there are multiple siblings, it is very likely that one of the kids will be deputized and placed "in charge" of the household and the other children until the parents return. Sometimes the kid in charge goes on a power trip and makes everyone miserable, often using the opportunity to take retribution for pre-existing sibling beef. Other times, the kid left in charge doesn't care and is occupied with their own interests. They let everyone run rampant throughout the house, fighting and breaking stuff.

Although I wasn't the oldest, I was often placed in charge. I remember wanting to do a good job with my duties by maintaining peace and making sure I was a fair judge should any disputes arise amongst the other kids. So today's message is actually about being a good steward of God's grace. When God's grace and mercy saved you, it didn't make you better than the next man or woman. It actually places a responsibility on you to be a good steward over the grace you were afforded. You're in charge of representing Christ in the earth until He comes back. I fear that we haven't done such a good job with this. So many people have been turned off from following Christ and His church because of the way that some of us have carried ourselves in His absence. Some are on power trips trying to use Christianity as a means of control. Others are so preoccupied with their own interests that they are too busy to care about the chaos all around. I encourage you to examine yourself today. What are you doing with the gifts and the grace that you've been given? Do you represent Him well?

READ TODAY: 1 PETER 4:10

DAY 139
YOU GOT ONE MO' TIME...

It's been said that warning comes before destruction. Well black folks are very good about issuing warnings before the consequences come down. One such warning is, "You got one mo' time...". Someone might say, for example, "You got one mo' time to get smart with me." If someone says this, I advise you not to test it. You never know who is crazy and hanging on by a thread. Should you decide to test the warning and perform the offense one more time, you'll just have to accept whatever comes next. You had an opportunity to chill, but you chose violence instead.

Thankfully, every morning that we wake up, God has given us at least one more allocation of time. Tomorrow isn't promised to anybody. So when we wake up, we should try to be intentional enough to put gratitude at the forefront (even if we don't feel like getting up and going to work). A new day means new mercy. We were allowed "one more time" even though we may not deserve it. Let's do our best each day to use our lives to serve the Lord with gladness. Let's put away the weighty encumbrance of sin and the works of the flesh. Just because God's mercy spared us last time, does not mean that we have unlimited time and mercy for consequences. You don't know how many more "times" you really have, so perhaps it's best to go ahead and yield to the will of God for your life instead. Our time is in His hands.

READ TODAY: PSALM 31:15

DAY 140
I'LL BEAT THE BLACK OFF OF YOU!

I am truly concerned by how many different ways we know how to threaten people. Hmm. Well anyway, today's phrase is very well known. If you want someone to know that you mean business, you may threaten them with the notion that you are going to beat them up so badly that the melanin leaves their skin!

Although people may have threatened to **beat** the black off of you, God is the opposite. He offers to **love** the black off of you. Of course we're not talking about our beautiful melanin here. We are talking about the darkness and the black stain that is sin. In the 51st Psalm, David pleads with God to purge, clean, and wash him to the point where he is whiter than snow. He isn't talking about an outward appearance here. He wants his very heart and soul to be washed clean. Imagine that! I love that for David because it shows his desire to separate himself from his own unrighteousness. He actually **wants** to be upright and Holy before God. That is significant because we are living in a time where we just want God to be cool about a little sin here and there, because we enjoy it. We're okay with being a nice shade of off-white. Slightly dimmer than snow, but close enough, right? Well, let me remind you that Jesus came to wash us and cleanse our hearts so that we could be forgiven and made free from the sin that once had us bound. So let's stop holding on to sin and grab hold to the freedom that is in Christ. Let Him wash you whiter than snow.

READ TODAY: ISAIAH 1:18

DAY 141
CUT YOU DOWN TO THE WHITE MEAT

Yo. I really want to know why we threaten each other so much. This should be studied. But I digress. If someone threatens to cut you down to the white meat, you need to run. They are threatening to cut you so deeply that your tendons, cartilage, and muscle will be exposed. That is a frightening thought.

I am reminded of God's word. I know you're probably wondering how the threat of a deep laceration wound reminds me of the word, but stay with me. I'm going somewhere. The Bible says that God's word is quick, powerful, and sharper than any two-edged sword. If you are stabbed with a two-edged sword, it's even worse than being stabbed with a knife, because both sides are sharp. You are getting two simultaneous wounds for the price of one. But why liken God's word to something so deadly? Well it's not the killing mechanism Paul is referring to in Hebrews. It's the ability to QUICKLY cut/split/separate one thing away from the other. The word helps us to separate the truth from a lie. It helps us discern the true spirit of a thing vs what it looks like on the surface. The word of God is the great divider. I don't know what decision stands before you today, but if something you are doing cannot pass through the powerful filter that is the word of God, it needs to be cut away and discarded. It has to line up with what God says! Oh, but you have to know the word for this to actually...oop...let me not step on the toes today! I'll be back tomorrow!

READ TODAY: HEBREWS 4:12

DAY 142
DON'T LET YOUR MOUTH WRITE A CHECK
THAT YOUR BEHIND CAN'T CASH.

This is yet another phrase often used as a warning. Some people get to talking so recklessly that they fail to count the cost of their words. If your mouth writes a check by cussing someone out, for instance, or by talking about someone's mother, please understand that you better know how to fight. I've seen way too many viral videos where a bully thought they could say anything to the "shy" kid just before getting mollywhopped and dragged to and fro upon the asphalt. Their mouth wrote a check, but the rest of their body had insufficient funds to cover it.

There are some things that you cannot afford to **say**, because you cannot afford to **pay** the cost of those reckless words. The Bible tells us that our tongues have power. We are made in the image of God, and His words carried enough power to create man and the whole universe. It stands to reason that our words also have the power to create and possibly destroy some things as well. This is why we must be so careful and intentional with what we say and with how we say it. I am learning that everyone doesn't deserve my words. I am learning that sometimes it's better to just delete that paragraph and type "ok." I am learning to speak more with my actions than with my mouth. The ability to control your tongue is an indicator that your walk with God is an authentic one.

READ TODAY: JAMES 1:26

DAY 143
TALKING OUT THE SIDE OF YOUR NECK

Some of you may know this as the hit song by Cameo that came out in 1984. Others of you may have become familiarized with the phrase through HBCU marching bands. To this day, it is a popular band number, known affectionately as "Neck." But what does it mean? A person who talks out the side of their neck is someone who will say just about anything just so they can have something to say. It doesn't matter to them if it's untrue, uniformed, or a straight up lie…they're just a'talking.

Do you know someone who talks out the side of their neck? It's very annoying. I'll tell you that Satan is the father of talking out the side of your neck. He makes all of these untrue, uniformed suggestions that are nothing more than lies. That's **all** he ever does. Please remember that Satan is neither omnipotent nor omnipresent. He is not all knowing. We give him credit for being more informed than he actually is. Nothing he says is the truth. He is the father of lies and is desperate to deceive you. He uses true sounding lies to confuse people. This is exactly why you must know the truth for yourself. The truth is what makes you free from the tricks and traps. Take today's message as a reminder to study the word more. We could all stand to do better with this. God's word will help illuminate the pathway of your life.

READ TODAY: JOHN 8:44

DAY 144
WHO DO YOU THINK YOU'RE TALKING TO?

Have you ever let your mouth slip when talking to a parent or other adult black person, such as a teacher? If you ever said something reckless or disrespectful, they would immediately begin acting confused. They would undoubtedly ask you who it is you **think** you're talking to, because "ain't no way" you are talking to **them** like **that**. It's not like nowadays when adults are scared of the children, and disrespect is tolerated. If you had the unmitigated gall to pop off at the mouth to an adult, it must have been a mistake/misunderstanding.

And that's exactly how we must be with the devil. When he tries to get in your ear to lie and make demonic suggestions, you really don't have time to listen and go back and forth with him. Excuse me?! Who do you think you're talking to? He must be confusing you with someone who *isn't* a child of God. You should have way too much word (and therefore truth) in you to even entertain that foolery. My parents never went back and forth with me as a child because they knew that I simply was not on their level. How foolish would it be for us to go back and forth with someone who is supposed to be under our feet? Next time a demonic thought or suggestion comes, ask yourself why the devil is even talking to you. Immediately rebuke it and him just like Jesus did when he fasted in the wilderness for 40 days. The devil tried to tempt him, but it failed because Jesus knew the word. We must be the same way.

READ TODAY: MATTHEW 4:1-11

DAY 145
I'LL GIVE YOU SOMETHING TO CRY ABOUT.

Count yourself to be blessed and highly favored if you've never heard this one. This had to be in the secret black parent handbook (that I somehow never received). If you got in trouble for one reason or the other and began to cry about it, often times your cry would be followed up by a threat. "I'll give you something to cry about..." was akin to Bobby Womack's song, "If You Think You're Lonely Now..." Our parents were telling us to either pull it together and hush up or face a whooping that was truly worth the tears. I always thought this was crazy, but it usually worked.

There was a time in the Bible where the people gave Jesus something to cry about. I'll make a long story short: Jesus was out on tour when He got word that His close friend, Lazarus, was very ill. Instead of leaving right away, he stayed two more days and then went to go see about Lazarus and his sisters, Mary and Martha. When Jesus finally got there, they told Him that Lazarus was already dead. Mary and Martha were salty and low-key blamed Jesus. They told Him that if He had gotten there sooner, Lazarus would not have died. Jesus saw everybody crying and carrying on, and He was so bothered that He started crying himself. The Bible says, "Jesus wept." The onlookers assumed that Jesus was grieved because He loved Lazarus so much.

But that doesn't make a whole lot of sense, because Jesus had been trying to tell them all along that Lazarus was going to get back up. He went in the tomb where they had laid Lazarus, prayed, and told Lazarus to come on out...and he did. So why do you think Jesus wept? I personally believe He cried because He saw the terrible effect that unbelief had on His friends. That is something to cry about. Having a lack of faith is a bigger deal than you know.

READ TODAY: JOHN 11:32-35

DAY 146
GO GET ME A SWITCH.

I'm sorry. Today's phrase should have come with a trigger warning. Some of you may have come up in the era of gentle parenting, but if you are of a certain age, there is a high chance you got whooped with either a belt or a switch as a means of discipline when you were a child. To me, the switch was scarier than the belt. It was literally a small branch from a tree or bush. Apparently, some of your mamas made you go outside and pick your own switch from the tree before proceeding to whoop you with it. I can only imagine the added anxiety of trying to find the branch that would be acceptable to your mama, while also trying to determine which one would hurt the least.

It's interesting to note that a fresh switch would often be more moist and therefore more flexible/pliable than the old one my mom would keep on top of the fridge. Neither one of them felt particularly good, but the older one would often be harder and more rigid. Sometimes an old, brittle switch would break mid-whooping. I am reminded of how we are all branches stemming from the True Vine that is Jesus. As long as we remain connected to Him, we are alive and can continue to be nourished. When impact happens in life, we are flexible and able to remain intact. Once you disconnect from Jesus, however, you are disconnected from your lifeline. When life hits, you are hard, brittle, and easily broken. Yes, I just preached about switches. God's word is everywhere if you just open your eyes and ears to the Holy Spirit.

READ TODAY: JOHN 15:5-7

DAY 147
HAND ME THE REMOTE, BABY.

This one is wild. Have you ever been in a completely different room, perhaps on a completely different level of the house, when you hear your name being called by mom or dad? You drop everything and run to the room, only to be asked to hand them the remote that was right there in the room with them and only slightly beyond their own grasp. It was annoying and confusing, but as a child, you just respectfully obeyed and then went back to whatever you had been interrupted from doing.

You're probably expecting me to turn this into some deep revelation. Well to be honest, I still don't understand exactly why they didn't just get the remote for themselves. I have some theories, but I don't fully understand it, and I don't have all the answers. I just stopped by to remind you that sometimes you have to obey God without knowing all the answers. Some of you are waiting until you know and understand steps A-Z before you will take step A. If that's what you're waiting on, you may never obey. I recently heard someone say that "slow obedience is no obedience." My God Today! Let your swift obedience be a demonstration of your faith. Just like we did with our parents, we must come running when God is calling us. When He calls you, it's for a purpose. We may not understand everything just yet, but trust and believe that God knows it exactly. His plans for you are good. Obedience could be the key that unlocks your very next door.

READ TODAY: ROMANS 8:28

DAY 148
I CAN SHOW YA BETTER THAN I CAN TELL YA.

If someone uses this phrase with you, it could literally mean anything depending on the context and tone. If it's used in a romantic context...va va vavoom! If it's used in the midst of a contentious argument, it could mean a threat of physical violence. If an unhappy spouse says this, it may mean they are headed to the divorce attorney to file papers. If an ambitious, hard-working, dreamer says this, they are about to do something great!

When it comes to this life of following Christ, you can show much better than you can tell. I've learned that people can and will say **ANYTHING**. I've seen people say "I love you" while going in a secret voting booth, and...you know, never mind. Just know that words can sound sincere when they are not. Be careful going into business or even marriage with a person based only on words. You need to know if that person is filled with the Holy Spirit. Some of you are frustrated (right now, today...) because someone who claims to love you does not show any fruit thereof. The truth is, they can't even love you without the help of the Holy Spirit. Stop spinning your wheels arguing, fighting, and trying to figure out why they can tell you, but always fail to show you. My child, my child... you're so focused on their broken promises. I've been there, and it is a sure way to remain disappointed and depressed. Instead, pray for that person to be filled with the Holy Spirit. You may have to fast on their behalf as well. But let me tell you, it's SO worth it.

READ TODAY: GALATIANS 5:22-23

DAY 149
YOU AIN'T GOT A POT TO P*** IN
OR A WINDOW TO THROW IT OUT OF.

My goodness! Let me apologize in advance if the title of this devotion offends anybody's sensibilities. Pray for me. The Lord is still working on me. But if you're not sure what this phrase means, it's referring to a person who is extremely broke and destitute. Their situation is so bad that they don't even have a pot to "relieve" themselves in. It goes on to say that this person is so broke that even if they somehow found a pot, they don't even have adequate living quarters that would allow for the proper disposal of their waste.

This makes me think about Joseph in the Bible. When his brothers kidnapped him and sold him into slavery, he didn't have anything. He had no pot, and he had no window. You know what? I take that back. Joseph did have something. He had a word from the Lord over his life, and he had a vision. My God Today! For Joseph, life (as he knew it) changed almost instantly when he found himself in a dark and lonely pit, betrayed by his own flesh and blood.

Well let me be the one to encourage you today. Because God's hand was on Joseph's life, they couldn't keep him down. Read his story. He went all the way from the pit to the palace. He had to start life from scratch with nothing, and yet Joseph ascended to a place of honor, authority, and influence. He attained a position that he might never have experienced had it not been for the betrayal of his envious brothers. The devil meant it for evil, but God used it to fulfill His purpose in Joseph's life. God has the power to transform any circumstance into a manifestation of His vision for you. Lawd! No wonder Satan is so mad all the time! Listen, you might not have a pot or a window right now, but never forget who God says you are and what God says you have!

READ TODAY: GENESIS 50:20

DAY 150
YOU DONE LOST YOUR MIND,
BUT IMMA HELP YOU FIND IT.

I know some of you may not be familiar with this phrase. As sweet as it may sound, it's actually a fairly serious threat. You may hear someone say this just before they issue a butt whooping to whoever had been acting as if their mind was gone. I guess it's implied here that the person would suddenly be enlightened by the experience of physical pain.

I'm so glad today that Jesus offers to enlighten us in a different way. You see, sin had us all in a chokehold and acting like we had lost our minds. And the truth is, sometimes it does take pain or some other uncomfortable consequence before some of us are willing to change our mind and walk away from our sinful desires. Well we (humanity) had lost our minds so badly that we actually deserved the death penalty all together. Thankfully, Jesus took our place when He suffered, bled, and died on the cross for our sin. He took the penalty so that we would have an opportunity to find our right minds again. I pray that you will accept the free gift of salvation and the overall transformation that comes when you renew your mind and adopt the mind of Christ as your own.

READ TODAY: ROMANS 12:2

DAY 151
BRING ME MY POCKA BOOK.

I know, I know. It's "pocketbook." If you're still not sure, this is an old school name for a purse. Sometimes our mothers or grandmothers would ask us to bring them theirs whenever they had to give us money or write a check for something. You could pick the purse up and bring it to them, but you weren't ever supposed to open it or go inside of it unless otherwise directed. To this day, my own husband refuses to grab something out of my purse for me, no matter how much I tell him it's okay. He'll go get it and bring it to me, and dassit! Some are even superstitious about purses. Sitting one on the ground is strictly forbidden, because it means that you'll be broke. I've seen people repeat and practice this superstition in church, which is wild.

Well you may recall that Judas, the disciple who betrayed Jesus, was the one in charge of keeping the purse (or money bag) for the group. Ironically, he was also a thief and stole from the bag often. We often hear stories of how people who have been trusted to look after the finances are the very ones stealing, embezzling, and mismanaging that money. I don't think it's a coincidence that the closer people are to money, the more greedy and shady they seem to become. Money can really change a person if they are not rooted and grounded in God. We see it happen to others, and we think, "I'm a good person. I would never do that." Well it takes more than being a good person. You have to be led, guided, and convicted by the Holy Spirit, or else you are susceptible to the same mistakes if placed in the right situation. Today's devotion is simply to remind you that we are supposed to make money, but money isn't supposed to make us.

READ TODAY: 1 TIMOTHY 6:10

DAY 152
THIS AIN'T BURGER KING.
YOU CAN'T HAVE IT YOUR WAY.

Black parents thought they ate with this one, I tell ya. They would use this phrase if one of their children had been bold enough to tell them what they did or did not want to eat for dinner. Actually, they'd use it on any occasion where they wanted to make it clear that we were not about to get whatever it was we wanted. We all know that Burger King's most famous motto is "Have It Your Way" (1974-Present). They have had several other mottos throughout the years, with the most recent simply being, "You Rule." Each motto has the same theme: you're in charge.

Well when it comes to God, He's not just a "burger" king. He is the king of kings! And I hate to be the one to break it to you, but you're not the one in charge. You can't always have it your way. Our ways are often flawed and contaminated by the desires of our flesh. Every now and then, all I want is to be able to use my petty clapbacks to get someone together real quick. But God will have me over here praying for that person instead! Where's the fun in that? I kid, I kid...well kinda. See how my flesh doesn't wanna do right? That's why I can't always have it my way. Eventually, we realized the importance of a balanced diet and were grateful that our parents didn't feed us nuggets, fries, and pizza every day. Who wants high cholesterol and clogged arteries by 25? Instead of throwing a temper tantrum like a toddler, it's best that we yield to the sovereign, omniscient instruction that comes from God. He's the one who can see down the street **and** around the corner. We must humble ourselves enough to trust Him with our outcomes more than we trust our flesh. If you live long enough, you'll find out that having it your way often gets you in more trouble than it's worth.

READ TODAY: 1 PETER 5:6

DAY 153
27-PIECE

If you don't know what a 27-piece is, don't feel bad. I didn't know either for a while. But a 27-piece is a hair weave set that comes with 27 pieces of hair that are short in length. You can use them to create a "quick weave" that resembles a short style, such as a pixie cut. I did a little research on YouTube, and it seems that some women achieve a really beautiful/natural look, whereas others...umm...do not. I think a 27-piece is cool, because it allows you to wear a short cut without actually cutting your own hair.

You may be wondering how in the world this is going to be a devotion. Well...let's see. Some women use a 27-piece because they prefer not to cut their own hair. There was a man in the Bible named Samson, whose mother made a vow to God that he would never cut his hair. This would be a sign of loyalty to God. Samson grew up and became the strongest, most physically powerful man there was. He kept his people safe with his strength by fighting off the Philistines. His hair (aka his loyalty to God) was the secret to his strength. Sadly, he started dating a woman named Delilah who spent the whole time trying to find out his secret. He finally let his guard down and told her that it was his hair. Delilah had it cut off while he slept. Samson lost his strength and his ability to protect his people. I said all of that to say, be careful who you trust! Ask the Holy Spirit to reveal any hidden agendas operating within your circle. If that friendship/relationship causes you to renege on your loyalty to God, run!

READ TODAY: JUDGES 16:16-19

DAY 154
BALLING ON A BUDGET

If someone says that they are balling on a budget, it means that they are doing things that rich people do, but at a lower price point that fits their finances. Take a trip to Miami for example. One person may spend 25K for a first-class plane ticket, five nights at a luxury hotel, designer bathing suits, a private yacht, shopping, and several five-star dining experiences. Someone else may catch a flight using their cousin's airline voucher, get a few friends to split the cost on an AirBNB, use the same bathing suits from last year, and buy groceries to cook their own meals while on the trip. They spent three days in Miami for a grand total of $279.47. At the end of the day, they both had a blast in South Beach.

Can you believe the Bible speaks about balling on a budget? That's right. We are invited to come eat, drink, and buy, even if we don't have money. How is that possible? It's God's personal invitation for us to take part in the riches of His glory **on His tab.** Whew! There's balling, there's balling on a budget, and there's something called getting sponsored. Let's thank God today for sponsoring us and allowing us to ball on **His** budget. Jesus has already paid for it all with His sacrifice on calvary. It's time for us to stop trying to pay for our own sin, because that leads to nothing but guilt, shame, condemnation, and eventually hell. Instead, accept the free gift/sponsorship that God has provided through His only begotten son. I promise the trip you take with Him will be far greater than anything you can afford on your own.

READ TODAY: ISAIAH 55:1-2

DAY 155
LET ME TELL YOU WHAT YOU AIN'T GON' DO.

Today's phrase is used mostly by the sisters. When someone tries to get away with doing or saying something whack, a black woman might be quick to jump in and tell them what they **ain't** gon' do. "Let me tell you what you **ain't** gon' do. You ain't gon' sit up here, eat up all my groceries on day one, and then holler that there's nothing to eat in the house!" This phrase extends to any type of trifling behavior from family, co-workers, politicians, or just the general public. Some people have a lot of audacity and little to no boundaries or sense, so sometimes you just have to inform them of what they are **not** going to do.

On the flip side, sometimes **we** have a lot of audacity and little to no boundaries or sense, and God has to tell **us** what we ain't gon' do. Has God ever told you no or not to do something? What was your response? The Holy Spirit will often let us know when we aren't supposed to be moving in a certain direction. Hmm...did something come to mind just then? If so, don't ignore it. It's not always easy, but we have to be bold enough to follow the guidance of the Holy Spirit even when we don't understand exactly why just yet. His "no" is often there to protect us from some danger that we cannot see. When the Holy Spirit tells you what you're "not going to do," I encourage you to listen. And if you're (genuinely) unsure, it's okay to pray and ask for confirmation and clarification.

READ TODAY: JOHN 16:13

DAY 156
YOU ACT LIKE YOUR **** DON'T STANK.

Today's phrase is used to describe people who either do not realize or refuse to acknowledge the things about them that are trifling. They walk around judging the messes of others as if they don't have mess of their own to be worried about. These people often look down on certain people and think themselves to be better than everyone else. Yes, I'm looking at you, bougie Thanksgiving auntie that throws shade at other family members every year to keep the heat off of yourself.

The Bible is very clear in letting us know that we **all** have sinned. The only person born into this world who had absolutely no sin was Jesus. So without God's grace and mercy, we would all be up the creek without a paddle. Some people have not searched their own hearts enough to know that their mess is indeed mess. Others know about their mess and pretend it's not there. But there is a third group that lies in what may be even more dangerous territory. These people feel as if they are clean, but that's only because they think they've taken care of their own mess. They feel that they pulled themselves up by their own bootstraps and that others should do the same. These people are self-righteous. They don't realize that we literally have no righteousness of our own. Any and all righteousness **must** come from God who imputes it onto us because of our acceptance of what Jesus did at Calvary. God is the only one who can take our poop and flush it away. Okay, I'm sorry for that visual. All I really want to do is remind us to stop testifying of ourselves as if we got it together on our own. Instead of giving ourselves the credit, we must point to what Jesus did and to what He enabled us to do through Him.

READ TODAY: ROMANS 10:1-3

DAY 157
GOTTA GET THIS MONKEY OFF MY BACK

If someone speaks of getting a monkey off their back, they are saying that they are struggling with a difficult issue that they really want to resolve. This is usually a problem that they have tried to fix many times unsuccessfully. No matter what they do, it seems like this "monkey" hangs on and follows them wherever they go. This phrase is often used in reference to some addiction. There can be a gambling monkey, a fried chicken monkey, or even a sex monkey.

If you haven't connected the dots yet, Satan is behind every monkey. He wants you to believe that the problem or addiction is too hard to fix, so it's better to just enjoy it while you can. He wants you to think that all you need is one more hit and then you'll be able to walk away using your own willpower. That's how he gets you stuck in the cycle, believing that every time will be your last.

The Bible tells us how to get the monkey off of our back. It says to "submit yourselves" unto God and to resist the devil so that he will flee. Submitting yourself to God is more powerful than any rehab center will ever be. Don't get me wrong, those places can be a blessing, but everyone doesn't have the luxury of checking into a facility because they can't seem to stop answering Rodney's booty calls. But just as you would check into the clinic, check yourself in with God. When you submit to Him, you are admitting that the problem is too much for you and that you're finally ready to do it His way. Some of us will resist God for years at a time, but whenever the devil says jump, we simply ask "how high?" Do you have a monkey on your back? Stop resisting God and start resisting that ugly monkey, the devil.

READ TODAY: JAMES 4:7

DAY 158
2-PIECE AND A BISCUIT

Okay, some of you may not know what this means. No, I am not talking about a fried chicken combo as ye suppose. A "2-piece and a biscuit" is commonly known to be a fighting technique. You throw one punch with the right (piece #1), one punch with the left (piece #2), and finish with another right, either to the body or as an upper cut (biscuit). If somebody offers you a 2-piece and a biscuit, please turn it down and walk/run away.

When it comes to the Lord, so many of His ways seem to go against our own human nature. This makes sense when we think about it, because He wouldn't be God if He was exactly like us. One such thing is how we should react when attacked. Human nature says we should respond by fighting back and defending ourselves. God says we should "turn the other cheek." Just the thought of that is wild to us. You mean to tell me if someone hits me with a right, I should turn and let them get me again with a left?

It sounds crazy, but God wants us to operate at a higher level than what our flesh would suggest. Anybody can fight back. Anybody can stoop to the level of an evil person. But it takes a personal relationship with the Lord to love your enemies and to pray for them. It takes more strength to see them how God sees them and not seek revenge. If people need to be punished or corrected, it's simply not our job. God can do it more effectively than you ever could. If someone tries to fight against you, you should pray for them and put it in God's hands.

READ TODAY: MATTHEW 5:38-48

DAY 159
NOW I JUST NEED SOMETHING SWEET.

Some people's tastebuds were programmed from an early age to eat desert after every meal. I wasn't one of those people. We grew up with so many kids in the house that desert just wasn't a priority. My mom didn't make sweets a normal part of my diet, so I don't eat them as much even as an adult. And I certainly can't eat them immediately following a meal. I know, it's weird. I always found it fascinating that people could complete a whole meal, be full, and still lean back and say, "Now I just need something sweet."

I may not need something sweet after my meal, but there is something sweet that all of us do need. In Psalm 119, we see where the psalmist refers to the Lord's very words as sweet. He says that they are literally sweeter than honey. I would have to agree. Just one word from the Lord can shift your entire life.

Have you ever heard God's voice telling you something encouraging? I have. It's one of the sweetest things ever. You feel so grateful that God took time to confirm something, give direction, or just remind you of His love. If your significant other says sweet things to you, that's awesome! But I can guarantee you that their strongest mack game doesn't compare to the sweetness of God's words to you.

READ TODAY: PSALM 119:103-104

DAY 160
NO ROOM TO TALK

If someone says that you have no room to talk, they just called you a hypocrite. They are saying that whatever or whoever you're speaking on is no worse than you are yourself. If social media hasn't shown me anything else, it's shown me that there are so many delusional people walking amongst us. And maybe I'm wrong for saying that. But how do you see a celebrity on Instagram enjoying a yacht in Miami and make a negative comment about how her booty needs a BBL, all while you're sitting at home with a backside that's flat as a pancake? Make it make sense.

If there's one thing Jesus did not appreciate, it was a hypocrite. He especially took issue with the religious hypocrites. How are you preaching one thing and living something else? To this day, we have hypocrites everywhere. Did you know that there are people who get online giving relationship advice to thousands of people, all while emotionally and physically abusing their own partner? There are even some pastors and preachers doing it too. The best thing to do is to honestly evaluate what's going on inside of yourself before you choose to open your mouth when it comes to others. Take care of home first.

READ TODAY: MATTHEW 7:3-5

DAY 161
FIGHTING WORDS

Fighting words are phrases that can potentially incite violence. If you say to me, for instance, "We are out of tacos…" I would consider those to be fighting words. Because what do you mean you're out of tacos?! How hard is it to get some tortillas and some…wait…see. There I go. Let me calm down. It's just a hypothetical situation. Whew. I was ready to fight somebody for playing with my hypothetical tacos.

The Bible teaches us about fighting words. Certain words, along with how you say them, can trigger anger. Sometimes that anger isn't even necessary. Have you ever gotten into it with someone only to realize at the end that you actually both agreed? This can happen when a person's tone is overly aggressive or even overly defensive. This is another reason why it's best to be quick to hear and slow to speak. That gives me time to process what is being said and choose the best way to respond, instead of launching into a kneejerk reaction where my tone matches your tone, and the next thing we know, there's a fight.

The Bible says that a soft answer turns away wrath, and this is true. Maybe it's my age, but I don't have the time, energy, or health to be going back and forth with people. Let's talk smarter, not harder.

READ TODAY: PROVERBS 15:1

DAY 162
PUT TWO AND TWO TOGETHER

This phrase is used when someone reaches a conclusion by piecing together the available evidence. "I finally put two and two together when I realized that Rico and Cheryl were always conveniently out of town at the same time." I don't know why we decided to use the number "2" out of all the available numbers, but that doesn't matter. What matters is that we finally connected some dots.

Has the Lord ever helped you to connect some dots in your life? In the world, they call it an "epiphany," but here in the body of Christ, we like to call it a "revelation." When God gives you a revelation, He uncovers (or reveals) something that was previously hidden from your understanding. When God helps you put two and two together concerning a matter, it's such an amazing, indescribable feeling. It feels like you've been crawling around in a pitch-black house, searching for a key to open the locked door to get out. Finally, all the lights come on, and you see the key that had only been inches away from you all along. Wait…okay, I guess it's describable. Anywho…the Bible tells us that we only have partial knowledge of things now. When the time comes for us to meet the Lord face to face, we will be able to see the full picture. Certain things in life may not make sense today, but God will put two and two together for you in His own timing, whether it be on this side or when we meet Him face to face. In conclusion, trust in God is essential if you want to keep from going crazy down here.

READ TODAY: 1 CORINTHIANS 13:9-12

DAY 163
POINT A TO POINT B

Point A to Point B is a very clear goal. Can the car get me from Point A to Point B? That's all the information that's required. If you ask this question, it means the car doesn't have to be fancy. It can be scratched and dented with no A/C, yet the goal remains the same. Will it get me from Point A to Point B?

Sometimes in life, the aesthetics simply don't matter. All that matters is whether or not you can travel from where you are now and arrive at the desired destination. There was one time in the Bible where Jesus healed a blind man by spitting on the ground, making a muddy substance, and then rubbing it over his eyes. As nasty as that process sounds, do you think that blind man cared? My boy was just trying to get from Point A to Point B. He went from full-on blindness to what I assume was perfect vision.

Sometimes God will take you through a process that isn't pretty. Don't let anybody discourage you from trusting Him. He is healing you and transporting you from Point A to Point B. Don't get caught up in how the process looks or even feels. Stay focused on the fact that you are blessed just to be in motion and moving in the right direction.

READ TODAY: JOHN 9:6-7

DAY 164
HOOPING & HOLLERING

There is some disagreement in the community on whether the phrase is "hooping and hollering" or "hooting and hollering." I'm not sure which is correct, but they are basically interchangeable. I remember my grandparents telling us to "stop all that hooping and hollering in there," if we as children got too loud in the next room. Whether we were in there jumping off the couch, arguing with each other, or just being loud and rambunctious, we knew it was time to turn down the volume.

A person who is hooping and hollering is making a bunch of unnecessary verbal noise. What unnecessary verbal noise have you been making lately? Do you like to argue? Do you have trouble resisting petty clapbacks? Must you always have the last word? Have you been complaining a lot? Perhaps you have been telling the wrong people all your business. Maybe you're quick to gossip and tell someone else's business. Well I'm here today to tell you to stop all that hooping and hollering. What if I told you that you can accomplish more with even fewer words than you're using? The Bible tells us that we should "study to be quiet." This tells me we need to apply intentional effort in order to keep ourselves from hooping and hollering. It takes practice, but we can learn to be more discerning about how, where, when, and why we use our verbal communication. If we must hoop and holler, let's let it be to God in prayer. I guarantee it will be much more productive. He will give us direction and wisdom on how to communicate well with the necessary words.

READ TODAY: 1 THESSALONIANS 4:11

DAY 165
WHEELING & DEALING

Let me tell you something about my people. If we can make something rhyme, we will! If someone is said to be wheeling and dealing, they are being compared to a casino. They are taking advantage of someone else's naivety in hopes of getting a "come up" themselves. They will reel someone in (usually made easy by that person's own greed or ambition) with a chance of easy money. Just like at the casino, this wheeling and dealing is really designed to benefit the wheeler and dealer. The house always wins.

And that's exactly how it is when we are tempted by Satan. I really don't care what he offers you, don't take it. It may look good, but I can guarantee that it's designed to benefit hell and not you. I know it looks like other people are taking the deal and winning the game, but please understand that things are not always as they appear. Think about all of these celebrities. What has been done in the dark is beginning to come to light for many of them. And for many others (celebrities and regular folk), there are private consequences taking place because they thought they could take the shortcut and win while playing on Satan's team. Please be patient. Any opportunities that come, be sure to pray and ask God if they come from Him. Don't be so thirsty that you allow Satan's wheeling and dealing to deceive you.

READ TODAY: MATTHEW 4:8-11

DAY 166
SKINNING & GRINNING

If you're not familiar with this term, it is used to describe a person who is smiling in your face in a way that is not genuine. Have you ever had somebody to do this with you? They come around acting as if y'all are best friends, knowing good and well they can't really stand you. They have absolutely no idea that you are already privy to what they said about you behind your back. And yet here they come, skinnin' and grinnin' in your face like a cheshire cat. Actually, that describes it perfectly. If you've ever seen *Alice in Wonderland*, you will recall that the cheshire cat was always smiling real big even though he was honestly just condescending and throwing shade the whole time.

As much as it hurts to discover that a friend is really a foe, I don't want to focus on them right now. Let's focus on ourselves. I'm going to teach you a new word that I picked up in Romans 12:9 in the King James Version. The word is "dissimulation." Dissimulation is the act of concealing one's true thoughts, feelings, or character. It means you are putting on a pretense. I know that some of us have to put on a happy, professional face for work, but is it turning you into a dishonest, disingenuous person? I want us to find a way to show love, kindness, and gentleness towards people (even when they annoy us), because we bear fruit from the Holy Spirit, and not because we've mastered being fake and phony. Anything else is dissimulation, and you are practicing to become and insincere individual overall. I **really** don't want that for you. Examine yourself to see if you may be lacking sincerity behind that smile. If so, it's time to strengthen your connection to the Holy Spirit. His fruit will enable you to smile, love, and care from a pure place and not from a place of manipulation. You may have to let this one simmer today.

READ TODAY: ROMANS 12:9

DAY 167
SNIGGLING & GIGGLING

This phrase refers to people who are laughing at someone in a mocking way. It's the definition of laughing **at** someone and not **with** them. I think of the times when kids get in trouble at school. While the "problem child" is being chastised by the teacher, there are usually a couple of girls in the back of the class laughing at their classmate's misfortune. The teacher will sometimes get on to them for it. "Uh...Kristen and Kim. You're next if you don't stop all that sniggling and giggling back there."

I hate to admit it, but I've definitely been guilty of sniggling and giggling. Sometimes I'll see a funny meme on social media, laugh, and forward it to friends, forgetting that there are actual people that those memes are making fun of. As you may have guessed, I'm not a super deep saint. I love to laugh, but I have to check myself to make sure that I'm not poking fun at another person's misfortune. The other day I saw a post about a man who had no neck. The comment section was nothing but joke after joke about this man's lack of a neck. I mean, the jokes were top tier. They were so clever that someone literally took the comments and turned them into a song. Yeah...the Holy Spirit convicted me for laughing. The internet has a way of desensitizing us to things that shouldn't be okay. I know God has a sense of humor, but I never want to get to a place where I am so desensitized that I laugh more than I pray. Truth be told, I'd rather laugh at the Diddy jokes than pray for him, and that is a shame. I know certain people don't seem as if they "deserve" our prayers, but that is a terrible position to take. We aren't God. If it wasn't for His grace and mercy, we could just as easily be in the same position as the person we are sniggling and giggling about. Let's repent today for any time where we either laughed or rejoiced at another person's situation.

READ TODAY: LAMENTATIONS 3:22

DAY 168
LOOKING LIKE WHO SHOT JOHN

This phrase is wild. I have absolutely no idea of its true origin. Some have theorized that the "John" in question is JFK. All I know is that if somebody looks like Who Shot John, they look a hot mess. I imagine that a person who looks this way has on mismatched clothing, dirty socks with slides on, and their hair is all over their head. I also imagine that their skin is dry and ashy, and perhaps they have crust around their eyelids.

Yup, you guessed it! Today's devotion is about fasting. Oh...you didn't guess that? Well either way, this is a gentle reminder that whenever you are fasting, you're not supposed to be walking 'round here looking like Who Shot John. When people walk around looking like the "woe is me, I'm fasting right now" archetype, they are defeating the purpose. This isn't the time to show everyone how much you're struggling, straining, and sacrificing for the Lord. This isn't the time to look for pats on the back. If you do that, those back pats will serve as your only reward. Rather, fix yourself up, put on some lotion, and carry on as you normally would. Your colleagues will just have to speculate as to why you didn't eat any of the random free cheesecake that magically appeared in the breakroom out of nowhere on the ONE day you couldn't have any, when you LOVE cheesecake! Oh, I'm sorry...triggered. What was I talking about? Ah yes...just let it be between you and God. He will see what you are doing in secret and will reward you openly.

READ TODAY: MATTHEW 6:16-18

DAY 169
LOOKING LIKE WHO DID IT AND WHY

Today's phrase is similar to yesterday's in that it describes a disheveled appearance. Saying that a person looks like "who did it and why" is like saying that this person looks like they don't even know what hit them. The person not only looks like a hot mess, but they look like a hot and confused mess. You want to see someone you haven't seen in years? Go to the grocery store looking like who did it and why, and I can guarantee that will be the time you run into everybody!

Has life ever dealt you such a seemingly unnecessary blow, that you never even saw it coming? You didn't even know who did it and why. All you know is that it left you hurt, confused, and looking crazy. Maybe you lost a loved one unexpectedly. Perhaps you had a boss who conspired to get you fired. Maybe you had a spouse who was unfaithful and left you to be a single parent. Perhaps you ate some bad Taco Bell at 11:46pm and found yourself fighting for your life on the bathroom floor at 3am. Well I want to remind you today that when attacks come, you **do** know exactly who did it and why. Don't get confused into thinking that you are fighting against these people you see every day. It's a battle that is taking place in the spirit realm. The worst thing you can do is be ignorant concerning "who" is doing it. You will be busy fighting your family, co-workers, and the lady in the Taco Bell drive thru, when you really need to be using spiritual tools like fasting, prayer, and praise. Once you remember the "who," don't forget the "why." You are an anointed man or woman of God. Of course Satan and his demons are threatened by you! They are doing their best to neutralize you in order to steal, kill, and destroy your God-given assignments. Don't fall for it!

READ TODAY: EPHESIANS 6:12

DAY 170
A GRIP

A "grip" is a well-known unit of black measurement. If anybody ever tells you that something was a grip, they are telling you that it was a whole lot. We often use this when referring to the cost of something. "You got front row tickets to the Usher concert? I bet that cost a grip!"

This is going to seem like a reach, but it's my book, and I'll reach if I want to! When I think about the phrase, "a grip," I am reminded of a king in the Bible named King Agrippa. We've mentioned this before, but in the book of Acts, Paul is brought as a prisoner before King Agrippa, and he ends up telling the king his personal testimony about how he had come to receive the gift of salvation through Christ Jesus. He preached the gospel in that moment, and it was so utterly compelling that King Agrippa famously stated that he was almost persuaded to be a Christian himself. But as my father used to say, "Almost only counts in horseshoes and hand grenades." Today, I want to talk to those of you who are not **fully** persuaded. Give God a try. Woe unto the person who hears the gospel preached and decides to ignore it. I challenge you to give God a real try in **every** area of your life. Pray and ask God to show Himself to you in an undeniable way. For those of you reading this page who are already fully persuaded, take this moment to pray for those reading it who are not. Let's pray that they will receive God's free gift **today**. It cost Him a grip. It cost His only begotten son, and it's the most valuable thing you will ever find.

READ TODAY: ACTS 26:28

DAY 171
WHO IS WE? THAT'S Y'ALL.

Have you ever had someone to lump you in with a group that you did not want to be lumped in with? For example, someone may say, "We don't like our food to touch." Another black person may respond by saying, "Who is we? That's y'all. I want my mac & cheese touching my sweet potatoes every time!" If there's one thing we don't like, it's being associated with a group that we truly do not want to be associated with.

Sadly, there are people sitting in jail right now, not because they committed a crime, but because they were with other people who committed one. That alone should speak volumes. The Bible warns us numerous times about entertaining the wrong kind of company. Foolish people can rub their foolishness off on you if you're not careful. Sometimes, as Christians, it is easier to blend in than to stand out. However, we are not called to just quietly agree with sin in our lives. I'm not talking about going around, judging others, and trying to force Jesus down their throats. I'm talking about **you** and your own life. When people try to lump you in with their sin, are you quick to separate yourself from it? We are called to be a light in dark places. Sometimes that will be uncomfortable, but you never know when your light is there to save someone's life. Let's pray and ask God for holy boldness, wisdom, and discernment to know how to embrace our distinguishing factors without shame.

READ TODAY: 2 CORINTHIANS 6:17-18

DAY 172
IF YOU BUY A MAN SHOES, HE'LL WALK OUT YOUR LIFE.

Of course I don't believe in superstitions, but there are plenty of black people who still dabble in them. I had never heard this one until a few years ago. But apparently, it's "bad luck" for a woman to give her man a pair of shoes as a gift. The superstition claims that the man will leave you as a result. It sounds completely silly to me, although I did actually go through a breakup shortly after gifting some sneakers that one time. Hmm. Nahhh.

Do you subscribe to any superstitions? Do you keep your purse off the floor for fear that you'll be broke? When your hand itches, do you think it's a sign of money coming your way? What about New Year's Day? Do you refuse to wash a load of clothes for fear that you'll wash one of your loved ones away? Do you eat collard greens on New Year's Day for good fortune? Or maybe you're the one who has to be wearing the team jersey and sitting on the right side of the couch for your team to win the game.

Let's leave superstitions to the people who don't believe in God. He's definitely not up there saying, "Well, I had ordained this awesome man to become Brandi's husband, but I'm so sorry…I changed my mind because she gave him some shoes for Christmas." The Bible speaks against believing old wives' tales and such. When we do this, it may seem harmless, but we are seriously undermining our own belief that God is fully sovereign. Our lives are in His hands. I know what your mama told you, but it's okay to make up your own mind that God's powerful hand is not limited by any superstition we may have been taught. Set your mind free today.

READ TODAY: 1 TIMOTHY 4:7

DAY 173
ONE MONKEY DON'T STOP NO SHOW

Now I don't necessarily condone calling people monkeys, but this phrase can be an absolute gamechanger. If you've ever been to a circus, you know that there are multiple moving people and parts. There are always several animals, including monkeys. I imagine working with monkeys can be difficult at times. They are susceptible to mood swings and may even be under the weather some days and unable to perform. But even with an unreliable monkey, I can guarantee you that the show will never be cancelled based on one monkey's absence.

Life is also full of moving people and parts. These people will come and go. Some will leave your life on their own accord, some will have to be escorted out, and others will only depart because of death. One major issue I see with many believers is the grief they deal with when loved ones are no longer there. I've seen grief-stricken people fall into bitterness, become depressed, and turn away from their faith, all because someone is no longer there. I've seen people get sick and even die because they can't move forward after losing someone.

Listen, Satan loves to use grief to keep you from your purpose here on earth. He will have you obsessing over that departed person for years, to the point of idol worship. Once you begin worshipping God's creation more than the Creator, you're in trouble. No one will tell you this because they don't want to hurt your feelings while you're in pain. But since I don't know you, I can say it. God is **sovereign** and doesn't make mistakes. No one can stay with you forever but God. He has a purpose and plan for your life, so please don't cancel the show. We are exposing Satan's tactics today because knowledge is power. It's a trick. Pray and ask God to heal your heart and your mind so that the "show" can go on.

READ TODAY: PSALMS 147:3

DAY 174
FIX YOUR FACE, OR I'LL FIX IT FOR YOU.

One thing about black parents back in the day, is that they simply didn't tolerate disrespect from kids. Most kids knew better than to pop off at the mouth, but some struggled in the area of their facial expressions. When an angry child (or adult, honestly) struggles to hold their tongue, sometimes it comes out as a twisted-up face. Well that twisted up facial expression is still considered to be disrespectful, especially if done in public. "Fix your face, or I'll fix it for you..." the parents would say.

Has God ever given you instructions that you didn't obey right away? Perhaps you knew you were supposed to end the relationship, but you weren't quite ready to let it go. Perhaps you knew you were supposed to put down the fried chicken, but you wanted to keep enjoying it a while longer. Maybe you were supposed to leave that job and start your business, but you weren't ready to lose the steady paycheck and health insurance. Well let me tell you, it's easier to just go ahead and obey quickly. Go ahead and fix whatever it is, because you really don't want God to have to start shaking things up to fix it for you. He'll allow the heartbreak and the dramatic breakup if that's what it takes. He'll allow the diabetes or the medical emergency if that's what it takes. He'll allow the company to lay you off if that's what it takes. But I want you to understand that it's only because He loves you and wants to see you victorious. He's only setting up those circumstances to help you win. Are you one of those people who has to hit the concrete before you obey? I don't want that for you. You can move much farther and much faster in life when you get out of your own way. Learn to trust God enough to let Him bless you without a struggle.

READ TODAY: LUKE 11:28

DAY 175
JUST GOING TO SHOW MY FACE

Have you ever been invited somewhere that you honestly did not feel like going? You knew, however, that your presence would mean a lot to the person who invited you. You wanted to show your support, so you made it up in your mind that you would go briefly enough to do just that. All you needed was for people to see that you came so that you could leave. In this situation, a person might say, "I'm just going to show my face."

Although that may work when it comes to friends and family, it doesn't work with God. When we show up in service to the Lord, we can't just do it to be seen doing it. We can't show up at church just so we can say we went. We can't just comment "I'm praying for you" underneath someone's post without actually going to God in prayer on their behalf. We can't do service in the community just to take pictures and be seen doing it. We can't just repost Christian-sounding memes on our social media but decline to open up the Bible and read it. You see, when it comes to God, He doesn't care about appearances. He looks directly at your heart to see your true motivation for doing (or not doing) things. If you find yourself going through the motions simply because you know you're "supposed to," then perhaps it's time to search your own heart to see what's really going on inside. Our works should be genuine and motivated by the overflow of God's love in our hearts. If it's not based on your relationship with Him, it's pointless. You don't want to meet God one day, only to be told that all you did was show your face, but never really knew Him. Take some time today to examine your heart and ask God to reveal anything in your life that isn't being done from a place of genuine love.

READ TODAY: MATTHEW 6:1-4

DAY 176
IF YOU FALL AND BUST YOUR HEAD,
I'M NOT TAKING YOU TO CHILDREN'S.

If your parents ever caught you doing something dangerous, such as climbing on top of the armoire so you can attempt to jump from there to the bed, you may have heard this phrase like I did. A simple, "get down" or "stop" wasn't going to be enough. They had to school you on the consequences and repercussions that would match your actions. "Aight now…if you fall and bust your head, I'm not taking you to Children's tonight!" This meant that if you did something dumb and got hurt, you'd just have to stay hurt, sad, and on your own, because they had absolutely no intentions of getting up, putting on clothes, and driving you to the hospital. Whether they meant it or not, the idea of being severely injured with no help was often enough to make you rethink your foolery.

Here's a thing I love about God. Even when the pain we are experiencing is a result of our own disobedience and foolishness, God is still faithful enough to get us the help we need when we need it. He doesn't leave us to suffer all alone. Yes, He warned us. Yes, He gave us an opportunity to think about the consequences to our actions. Yes, we "jumped off the furniture" anyway, fell, and hurt ourselves. It's painful and embarrassing, but here is the lesson. Don't allow your guilt and shame to keep you away from God's help! He's willing to accept your changed mind, forgive you for your foolishness, dress your wounds, and heal your broken heart. The devil wants you to think that God is so mad at you and so far away from you that you can't even pray to him. The devil is a lie. Thank God for grace! The Bible says that the Lord is actually close to those who are brokenhearted. In those moments, don't be so deceived that you forget to look to the hills from whence cometh your help. Your help comes from the Lord!

READ TODAY: PSALMS 147:3

DAY 177
A'HEHE HELL

Let's see. How do I explain this here phrase? If you find yourself laughing at something that isn't meant to be funny, you might hear this phrase used sarcastically in response. Honestly, I can't explain it, so let's just role play a bit.

Person A: Sheila told me I'm not invited to the cookout because I reneged playing Spades last time!
Person B: Oh that's funny! Bwahahaha! Hehehehe!!!
Person A: A'hehe hell! I'm pulling up to get my burnt hotdog, regardless!

Okay, let's talk about hell today. I know it sounds bad, but somebody needs to explain this clearly. It's a common misconception that good people go to heaven and bad people go to hell. That's not true. My pastor says that hell is a place for people who decided to pay for their own sins, but heaven is a place for people who decided to let Jesus pay. The Bible tells us that the **righteous** will inherit everlasting life. But that's where some can get confused. We oversimplify that word righteous to mean "being a good person." Yet there is no way that any of us can be considered righteous by God based on being "good" enough. So God decided that He would take our faith/belief in Him and credit it back to us as righteousness. We have no righteousness on our own. Sin has made us all like filthy rags. We only have the righteousness that was attributed to us by God's kindness in return for our faith in Him. So I need the saints to please stop walking around scared about going to hell. If we believe on the Lord Jesus, that He took the penalty for our sin and paid our sin debt in full, heaven belongs to us. If you reject Him, then okay...you have hell to think about. But once you believe and accept God's free gift, your focus should now be on fulfilling God's purpose for your life on earth. If the devil can trick you into thinking your performance can get you into heaven, you'll waste years being an ineffective believer. That's why it's important to know and read the word for yourself. Don't let anyone use it to control you with fear.

READ TODAY: MATTHEW 25:46

179

DAY 178
DRAW BACK A NUB

This expression is so funny to me, because I remember hearing it numerous times before I actually understood what it meant. I thought it was a metaphor for something else, but nope. It's literal. If someone tries or threatens to hit you, you may say, "Try it again, and you'll draw back a nub!" This means that if they attempt to stretch their hand or other appendage out to strike you, it will literally be gone by the time they draw it back towards themselves. The only thing remaining would be a nub or a stub.

Let's talk about that time when Peter was in the Garden of Gethsemane with Jesus as He was preparing himself to be crucified. When the soldiers came to apprehend Jesus, Peter was not having it. He drew his sword and swatted at one of the men, cutting off his ear. The man tried to come for Jesus, but thanks to Peter, he drew back a nub! But let me tell you what my Jesus did. He touched the man's nub and restored it! Jesus healed someone who was **clearly** his opp (for the older uncs and aunties, an opp is someone who **opp**oses you, also known as an enemy). Then Jesus rebuked Peter for "living by the sword."

But what was the point of that whole situation? What if the Lord wanted Peter to know that it wasn't his job to cover Jesus, but it was Jesus's job to cover for us. The Bible tells us that He didn't come to earth to be served by us, but rather to serve us. When Jesus healed the soldier, he kept Peter from getting charges and a possible death penalty himself. He stood in the gap for Peter and kept Him from having to pay for that sin with his life, just as He has done for each of us! I don't know. Maybe that's what it meant, maybe not. But either way, it's a good reminder today of how much Jesus loves us.

READ TODAY: MATTHEW 20:28

DAY 179
THE STREET COMMITTEE

The Street Committee is a very committed group of individuals existing in virtually every community. They are a self-appointed committee dedicated to the propagation of other people's personal business throughout the streets. If you've ever seen the sitcom 227, you may remember a committee member named Pearl who spent most of her day sitting in the window, ear hustling/eavesdropping. She really had her ear to the streets, so to speak. She would ascertain people's personal information and spread it to the rest of the street committee via gossip.

Are you a part of the street committee? Do you feel like it's your job to spread people's personal business in the streets? Do you participate in gossip and talk negatively about people behind their backs? We've all done it before. Who are we kidding? It can be more entertaining than watching the Jerry Springer show in the 90s. There are numerous scriptures that speak against the giving and receiving of gossip. But let me tell you this: it's no fun when the rabbit gets the gun. That means it's all fun and games until it's your name in those streets. If someone gossips to you, they will gossip about you. You don't want to sow those kinds of seeds. When I went through my divorce, there were people who I barely knew having conversations about me and my situation. They were judging me based on sketchy information from the street committee. I only know now because a couple of them eventually came to me and apologized for misjudging my character. It was a difficult time, but I learned to rise above the chatter and be the strong blllllack woman that I am today. Still, I don't think anyone should have to go through that type of emotional distress. Keep your heart and mind pure and keep your hands clean. I know the tea is piping hot, but it's also poisonous. We can't drink it anymore. Preaching to me.

READ TODAY: 1 TIMOTHY 5:13

DAY 180
I KNOW MY STUFF AIN'T JUST GET UP AND WALK AWAY.

This phrase is what you say when you are unsuccessfully looking for one of your belongings and begin to suspect that someone around you may have stolen it. You know you're not crazy, so you look at the person you suspect the most and say, "Now I **know** my stuff ain't just get up and walk away." The phrase is very accusatory in nature and will almost always offend someone, even if they are indeed guilty.

Okay, so think about your life. How are you doing today? How would you say life is going for you overall? I hope your answers to those questions were upbeat and positive. But for some of you, I know they weren't. Things can get hard at times, and it often seems like everything is happening to you all at once. Do you struggle to get to sleep some nights because there are so many concerns running around in your mind? Are you noticing an unexplainable decline in your overall health? Do you feel like you're constantly in a tug of war for no real reason? Well it sounds like maybe you've lost your peace, and perhaps you've misplaced your joy as well. But where did it all go? You used to have those things, right? I **know** your stuff didn't just get up and walk away!

It's true. Your joy and your peace **didn't** just get up and walk away. You voluntarily forfeited it without even realizing what you were doing. When life happened and your best solution was to take matters into your own hands, you were the one who got up and walked away. Your joy and your peace are exactly where you left them. You see, people don't get and keep joy and peace just because. Joy and Peace are fruit from the Holy Spirit that require you to stay connected to God, the True Vine, to get perpetual nourishment and thrive. He is our source and solution for **everything** life throws our way. Reconnect today, and let God help you locate those things which you lost.

READ TODAY: ROMANS 14:17

DAY 181
YOU BETTER TAKE SOME OF THAT BASS OUT YOUR VOICE WHEN YOU'RE TALKING TO ME.

There comes a time in a young boy's life where puberty hits, and he begins to change into a young man. One of the major changes is in his voice. He goes from a higher pitched, squeaky voice, to a deeper voice that contains a bit more bass. As the boy continues to grow, there's this awkward state of limbo where he's beginning to exhibit certain "grown-man" characteristics physically, but mentally he is still a child. As you can imagine, this can be a time of great conflict between parents and their sons. In the heat of a disagreement, a parent may use this phrase to remind their child to adjust their tone to a more respectful one.

Physical growth brings about a change in your voice, and spiritual growth should do the same thing. You can literally tell if a boy has hit puberty based on what he sounds like. Similarly, spiritual maturity has a distinct sound as well. Can people listen to you speak (or not speak) and tell that you've grown spiritually? Or do you sound the same as you always have? I'm concerned about followers of Christ who aren't growing and don't think they need to. We will never reach a place where we don't have room to learn and grow. We are on a continuous journey, and the journey itself is the real gold mine. That's why I'm glad you read this book. You took a great step by prioritizing your spiritual growth. You shouldn't sound the same way you sounded six months ago when you began. But please don't stop here! 6 months from now, I want you to have even more bass (wisdom, knowledge, authority, strength, and love) in your voice. We are lifetime learners over here. We'll never be perfect, but we can learn how to operate from a place of victory in Jesus in every area of our lives. I am praying for you, and I ask that you pray for me as well. Thank you for reading! Keep going! -Lori

READ TODAY: 1 CORINTHIANS 13:11

THANK YOU!

Thank you so much! Your love and support means everything!
-Lori

P.S. Link with me on IG @eyeslor and @mygodtoday

Why am I still talking? The book is over now.

Why are you still reading?

Y'all are my friends in my head. Okay, bye!

Did you know I have other books too? Yup.

Any of y'all know Oprah? Can you slide her a copy?

Okay, what about Jenifer Lewis? That's my Auntie in my head. I just want to meet her one day. Who has the hook up?

You're still reading? Hmm.

Do y'all really think Whitley should have married Dwayne that day? I think she should have got somewhere and saddown and prayed first.

Anybody like tacos?

Made in the USA
Monee, IL
03 January 2025

75865014R00111